RUNN

A COMPLETE BOOK ON HOW YOU CAN RUN FASTER EFFORTLESSLY TO GET FIT AND LOSE WEIGHT WITH EASY TIPS AND TRICKS

ERICK FOSTER

1

Disclaimer Notice:

Please note the information contained within this document is for educational and entertainment purposes only. All effort has been executed to present accurate, up to date, and reliable, complete information. No warranties of any kind are declared or implied.

Readers acknowledge that the author is not engaging in the rendering of legal, financial, medical or professional advice. The content within this book has been derived from various sources.

Please consult a licensed professional before attempting any techniques outlined in this book.

By reading this document, the reader agrees that under no circumstances is the author responsible for any losses, direct or indirect, which are incurred as a result of the use of information contained within this document, including, but not limited to, errors, omissions, or inaccuracies.

TABLE OF CONTENT

INTRODUCTION

If you've ever started running only to find yourself unzipping your shoes a couple of minutes later, welcome to the club. Every experienced runner, including, has gone through that phase not made for racing.

But people cannot be divided into those who can run and those who simply aren't made to hit the pavements. Everyone can achieve the stamina to become a marathon runner. The trick is knowing how to take the journey of running the right way.

Fortunately for you, this is the best place to start. Reading this book will give you all the right information and give you a couple of tricks up your sleeve for when training gets more difficult.

From why and how you should run to teaching you the ultimate technique to improve your running performance and become the athlete you've always wanted to be, this book is the only running guide you'll ever need.

Having the answers to all the questions new runners have, as well as clearing up the confusions and misconceptions that go hand in hand with running, this is the only guide that has the power to push couch potatoes into the world of fitness.

Are you one of those who need to get up and go? If so, click the "buy" button and join me on this fitness run.

Chapter 1: Essential information to get started

Running is the favorite activity of millions of people around the world. It's advantageous, plus it's cheaper than going to the gym.

Before getting started, buying running shoes is a must. The best thing to do is to buy running shoes at a store that has sports equipment. The staff are knowledgeable and can recommend the best shoes for some people's foot type.

There are three main types of feet:

• Flat feet - have dropped arches, so they are flexible and pronated to over pronation. Pronation occurs when weight is transferred from the heel to the forefoot and the foot rolls inward.

• Neutral feet - is the most common type of feet. The runner lands on the heel and rolls forward during the gait cycle until the impact is evenly distributed across the forefoot.

• High feet - are the opposite of flat feet. When the arches are defined the feet end up being stiff, this leads to supination. Supination represents insufficient inward roll of the feet after landing.

Keeping in mind the different shapes of the feet, shoe companies have begun to develop models to adapt to every type of foot. Choosing shoes designed specifically for a certain type of foot reduces the chances of injury.

Although minimalist inspired barefoot footwear is in fashion nowadays, it is not recommended to buy this type of shoe. Before buying minimalist running shoes, it is recommended that you wear a "step-down" shoe first.

A "step-down" shoe is minimal, but there is still slight support to the midsole. It is recommended that you buy these shoes because runners shouldn't go from a solid and stable shoe type to a minimal shoe type. Wearing minimal shoes requires bones, muscles, tendons and ligaments to strengthen and adapt. Most coaches advise against wearing this type of footwear for every run.

When buying, runners should always choose a pair of shoes that looked like part of their feet when they were trying them on.

After the new running shoes have been purchased, runners should introduce them. It is recommended to walk for a few days wearing new footwear. Feet will get used to the new sneakers and running will be more fun.

When the shoes are purchased and the necessary running equipment is ready, it is important to decide when to run. Runners should always strive to run around the same time each day.

Exercise experts constantly discuss the best time of day to run. A lot of research has shown that the optimal time to run is when your body temperature is at its highest. For most people, body temperature is at its highest between four in the afternoon and five in the afternoon. Other research has concluded that runners perform best between 4pm and 7pm.

However, morning runs are also useful. Running in the morning keeps the runner motivated. Morning exercises were shown to be more consistent with their regimens than people who chose late afternoon or evening runs.

Although people have a natural tendency to run better in the late afternoon or evening, the body can adapt to running in the morning as well. The runner should choose the best time based on their plans and abilities. Additionally, they should stick to the schedule for optimal results from their running.

In addition to footwear, there are other essential items for running:

- Clothes - should be made of technical fabric. This type of fabric helps runners stay dry and comfortable in cold, wet weather. It is of great importance to avoid cotton. When cotton gets wet, it stays wet, but breathable synthetic material like DryFit, CoolMax, etc. It wicks sweat away from the body and keeps it warm and dry during the winter.

- Running socks - shouldn't be made of cotton. The best socks are those made of synthetic material such as polyester or CoolMax.

- Water - because staying hydrated is extremely important. It is recommended that you drink four to six ounces of water every twenty minutes while running.

- Identity card and money: because every runner must stay safe while running outside. Therefore, having money in an emergency is very important.

- Running watch - is meant for timing races. While there are great running watches that measure a runner's heart rate and have many other functions, it's not really necessary. A regular watch with start and stop buttons is more than enough to time runs and compare progress every day.

- Sunscreen - should be applied regularly. Runners spend a significant amount of time outdoors, so the right sunscreen is very important. Sunscreen should be waterproof and should have an SPF of at least 15. In addition, the ideal sunscreen should offer a broad spectrum of protection (against UVA and UVB rays).

Now, when the equipment has been purchased and the run time is scheduled, you are good to go. Here are some rules every runner should follow while running outdoors:

- Don't take up too much space: When running in a group or alone in a busy area, don't force other runners, cyclists or pedestrians off the course.

- Stay Right: You should stay by your side and be very careful when turning left into a fast lane. Pay attention to cyclists and other runners.

- Follow Usage Rules: In case you operate in a place that has strict usage rules, be sure to follow them. If the rules are not posted, ask someone before starting the race or just do what they do. Usually, slower runners and hikers use the outside lanes.

- No loud music - while listening to music is a great motivator and helps people focus, you shouldn't turn the volume up to the max or take out a headset. You should do this in case there are obstacles in the way. You should be able to feel what is happening around you.

- Reporting is important: if you need to lace up your shoe or decide to walk for a while, move and report if there are other runners behind you.

- No waste: when you drink all the water or eat a whole bar, don't throw anything on the ground.

- Look both ways, especially at intersections, for your safety.

Chapter 2: Why Run?

You have undoubtedly heard that running is one of the best exercises for losing weight, getting fit and maintaining a healthy physique. However, running may seem like the worst thing you can do to your body when you're panting like a dog and you tear your lung apart. So why in the world would you want to start running, an exercise that sometimes seems to be more of a problem than it's worth?

The hardest part of the race is getting started. If you're new to running and feel like you don't know where to start, it can feel overwhelming, especially if you don't have a friend who has been doing it for a long time already. However, you might be surprised to know that after the first few tries, the ride becomes much more comfortable and can make you feel like a million bucks.

These general reasons for running are enough to get most people out the door. But that may not be your case, and that's okay, we're just getting started. There are many other reasons to go beyond that I guarantee you will have you running for your shoes. You just need that first reason to go out. Once you find the motivation to start life as a normal runner, it becomes a lot easier to start your journey.

Mental benefits

Unless you are experienced in running, you may not know that running is very beneficial for your mental health. When you feel like dying or can't catch your breath during a run, it can be hard to believe that your mind is actually getting healthier with each exercise, but it's true. In fact, mental benefits are the main reasons people keep running throughout their lives.

So what exactly does racing do for your mind? Studies have shown that running can affect both mental illness and general exhaustion. Running allows people to overcome difficult obstacles in life by forcing them to act outside of a stuck mindset. With the power to overcome adversity, the body becomes more readily available for difficult challenges, making your life much more enjoyable.

Execution decreases depression

Depression is one of the most difficult mental illnesses to overcome and is one of the main reasons runners have come up with. Depression can feel like a cage you can't escape from. After all, if you suffer from depression, it feels like the world is against you and the only place to feel safe is under the covers. Mental illness makes motivation difficult, so running can seem like the last place to find refuge during an episode.

However, if you find the energy to get out of bed, there are exceptional benefits to putting on those running shoes and getting out. Runners get what's known as a double pack of benefits. Not only do they receive the benefits of exercise, but they also receive benefits from being in nature. Unlike many other exercises, running can take you anywhere, making you a great way to stay in touch with nature.

Fresh air and sunlight are key to becoming a happier and healthier person. As depression causes its sufferers to remain in the shadows, the energy of an enclosed environment inevitably plays a role in that feeling of entrapment. A change in the environment has been shown to increase the moral and general happiness of those suffering from mental health problems. Vitamin D is one of the most common benefits of spending time in the sun, so wearing a pair of running shoes will allow you to get that needed vitamin for free.

Many non-runners also feel a sense of entrapment in this activity. They feel like beating the floor is lonely and hardly the place to cool your body if there is no emotional or physical contact with others. However, the running community is vast and always open to new people. Running doesn't have to be alone. In fact, many use running as an excuse to go out and meet new people. Running is often a way of life for people, so most are happy to get anyone involved in it.

Those with depression often also experience an emotional attraction, which makes their bodies feel nervous. Running impulses and energy in the muscles are common effects of depression. Running helps relieve those sensations by removing bad energy from the body. When you run, your body has the ability to move energy in a healthy way. The body becomes able to release tension and any emotions that drag you down or loosen your grip on reality.

Runners also often receive an added incentive to perform in the form of a runner's high. Often seen as a myth, a runner's high doesn't get the recognition it deserves when it comes to possible aids to depression. However, it is far from a myth. In fact, it was born from millennia of evolution for one purpose: to help the body overcome the aches and pains that come from excessive exercise.

There are three possible reasons for the runner's high. The first includes the theory that useful chemicals are released, such as dopamine, serotonin, and norepinephrine. These chemicals release feelings of happiness in the body, making running a lot easier. The second theory deals with the body's natural temperatures and its change positively affects our mood. The third explanation for the runner's high is the release of a chemical called an endocannabinoid. Yes, you read that right. Some believe that the runner's high distributes a compound associated with marijuana. So, when you go out on the track, you give your body a healthy alternative to drugs, literally.

Relieves anxiety

Anxiety is one of the most common forms of mental illness in the United States. One study concluded that nearly one in five people have been diagnosed with an anxiety disorder. And this statistic only applies to people who are diagnosed with mental illness, as a third of those come forward.

Anxiety causes a loss of focus and leaves the body in a constant combat or flight mode that prevents the brain from functioning properly. In a combat or flight mode, all the blood that would have been reserved for brain function is now used in other parts of the body, which can often be felt in the form of heart palpitations. As a result, the brain is often left with little blood flow, causing dizziness, panic, insomnia, and obsessions, just to name a few.

But what does this have to do with running? Like depression, anxiety causes brain hormones to overproduce or fail to produce certain chemicals that cause healthy brain function. However, running causes the body to produce these chemicals as it hammers the floor. Endorphins, or the "feel-good" chemicals in your body, are produced due to high rates of metabolic activity. So, the harder you work, the more likely you are to get these endorphins.

Another study suggests that improving telomere length plays a significant role in relieving stress. Telomeres are small particles in the body that prevent the chromosomes at their ends from fraying. Essentially, they act like plastic caps on the ends of chromosomes. The length of these telomeres determines the health of the body. Consider the needles at the ends of the shoelaces. While they may not seem like the most important parts of the lace, they actually provide a sturdy protective barrier that keeps your laces intact. Now consider their lengths. Extremely short needles are hardly useful with braided shoelaces and often break, causing the shoelaces to fray. The long needles, on the other hand,

Telomeres at the ends of chromosomes follow the same principle. Telomeres typically shorten over the years, which means they are linked to aging. Shortened telomeres lead to health problems such as stress. However, even a short period of intense exercise can help lengthen the telomeres, effectively acting as a healing agent. According to Elizabeth Fernandez,

"Intense physical activity of just 42 minutes over three days, similar to federally recommended levels, can protect individuals from the effects of stress by reducing its impact on telomere length" (2010). The greater the activity, the greater the chances of mental health. Running, as one of those vigorous exercises, plays a vital role in improving mental health.

Enhance learning

The brain receives more blood to the brain when the body stops focusing on a fight or flight mode and instead relieves the tensions built up by anxiety and depression. It would just make sense, then, that the extra brain blood from running would affect how you learn. You are able to remember details better and the mind can go back to its endorphin production.

In an experiment conducted by Bernward Winter, running was used as a method by which to determine the effects of exercise on the brain. All subjects were tested both before and after completing an intense running exercise. Before running, the bilingual subjects were asked to translate a sentence, a memory and an attention. They were then subjected to running on a treadmill with an increase of 1.2 mph after every minute. They ran until they were tired and resumed testing. The results showed a significant increase in cognitive speed (Winter et al., 2007). The bilingual subjects were able to translate at an accelerated pace and were able to better retain the words they learned after the exercise.

Other studies related to subjects' brain function have determined that running is one of the best ways to improve one's health. Hence, not only is aerobic exercise highly effective in improving learning and memory, but running provides an affordable option that is highly accessible and yet highly profitable. Candace L. Hogan determined, "Evidence of the benefits of exercise on both affective experience and cognitive performance indicates that exercise is an effective, low-cost intervention to improve both emotional and cognitive health." Brain health is determined, therefore, by how the body is used.

Since only a short amount of exercise has been shown to produce impressive learning results, just imagine how much continuous activity it can do for the mind and body. When you start running, you don't need to run six miles on the first day. Instead, work up to longer periods and you will see improvement in brain function over time.

Prevents brain aging

You see it in everyday life. The brain tends to age considerably over time, and many brain functions slow down. Since the increase in telomeres due to fitness prevents the body from aging rapidly, it makes sense that the brain also sees some resistance to aging.

A study recorded in Time Magazine in 2012 determines the validity of the suggestion that exercise stops or reduces brain shrinkage. Scottish scientists tested over 600 people in their 70s, asking them about their habits, including physical exercises and brain games.

They then performed MRI scans of all participants and noted the habits they had. Three years later, they brought new MRIs and recorded the exercises and brain games each participant mentioned. Those who were more active mind and body showed a reduced rate of contraction.

What is surprising about the study, however, is its connection to exercise. Although both exercise and brain games reduced brain shrinkage, exercise was determined to be the most important factor in retaining brain matter. Simple exercises like walking have been shown to help the brain maintain its high level of function.

Those who exercised the most showed the most improvement in brain function and the least shrinkage, meaning that more intense aerobic exercise proved to be the most beneficial. Even as a running beginner, you can reap the benefits of a healthy mind through determination and commitment to sports.

Helps heal the brain from substance abuse

Substance abuse is one of the hardest obstacles in any person's life to overcome. Many who start cannot break free from addiction the first or twentieth time. Cravings are some of the most intense sensations associated with substance abuse, and something as small as seeing condensation on the outside of a cold beer can cause relapse.

For those struggling with substance abuse, it can be very difficult to overcome the constant need for a stimulus. And this is where running can help. The high experienced while running can act as an alternative to simulated drug highs. Dopamine is one of the most effective natural chemicals in the brain that makes the mind feel "happy" and the most commonly produced by drugs. Running also produces dopamine and other chemicals, as a natural alternative.

Studies have shown that running has been shown to be effective in countering the effects of drug use. Dr. Wendy Lynch used this principle when working with cocaine-addicted mice. She and her team exposed the rats to a large supply of cocaine, creating addiction to each subject. Each cage was equipped with a cocaine supply lever which, if pushed, would distribute the drug. After the addiction, she cut their supply for two weeks. The control group was not allowed any form of stimulation or anything else that would help them release their frustrations. The test group was given a wheel in which they were allowed to run for two hours a day.

Rats that had access to a racing wheel showed a remarkably large improvement compared to those that did not. It was documented that they pressed the lever 35% less than the control group. When cocaine was reintroduced into the group, those with the wheel in motion pressed the lever 45% less than those without the wheel (Daniloff, 2017). The results indicate that both groups of rats, exposed to the same amount of cocaine, had radically different results based on one test difference: running.

Another study conducted for marijuana addiction showed more or less the same results. Each subject, 12 in total, described themselves as a marijuana addict and expressed no desire for rehabilitation. For two weeks, Dr. Peter Martin required each subject to run on a treadmill for 10-30 minutes each day. By the end of the first week, she saw a noticeable change in addiction levels, noting that their cravings dropped by 50% (Boerner, 2011). Although the experiment ran for two weeks, Dr. Martin stated that there was no need for further work after one week. The results of the race had proved themselves.

Running is far from the only way to deal with addiction, but it has proven to be one of the most effective. The brain is essentially rewired with each run to become more capable of dealing with the effects of difficult drug addiction. While running, the body becomes less dependent on external sources and instead focuses on the natural chemicals produced by the brain.

Many addicts use running as an outlet for cravings and other addictive behaviors. In fact, some rehabilitation centers actually use running as a method of overcoming drug addiction. Some facilities in the United States, Canada, and Ireland require "extreme" addicts to train for running competitions as part of their treatment. Even people who start recovery by running often see the benefits throughout their lives. They keep running, even though many of their regular cravings for their favorite medications have largely subsided.

Enhance creativity

Just as running can improve brain function, it's also essential to creatively connect the dots. Some of the most famous writers, painters and artists believe that walking or running significantly improves their ability to think. The brain reacts favorably to running and often creates new connections in the brain, leading to understanding and creative intelligence.

Through research, scientists have established that the creation of new cells is related to exercise. Exercise also improves the lifespan of those brain cells. As discussed earlier, the brain experiences improved brain function and health when exposed to exercise, and memory improves with higher levels of aerobic activity. The hippocampus shows an increase in size with regular exercise.

That's a lot of information, but it all comes down to one simple explanation: The brain has improved dramatically with aerobic exercise. The hippocampus is where creativity resides, so the bigger your hippocampus, the more likely you are to think both logically and creatively. After all, who wouldn't want a bigger brain?

Since running also helps those with anxiety and depression, it has become a key factor in creativity. Anxiety and depression bog down the mind with debilitating thoughts, but those that run often feel those negative feelings vanish when healthy chemicals are introduced into the brain. The mind can then become clear, allowing the mind to focus on creative pursuits.

Consistency is also the key to a happier brain. While taking time to run is a marketable achievement, developing a schedule for your workouts can improve your creativity over time. Author Haruki Murakami uses a routine to help him write some of his best work. If you've read one of his novels, then you know they are intricate and long. He spends several hours each day writing, then runs at least 6 miles or swims (Presland, 2017). He attributes much of his success to running because it helps him open his mind.

Those who struggle with creativity can see a potential increase in brain activity after a workout. With that in mind, it doesn't seem logical to give up a day from the gym. Although you believe you are primarily the left brain, studies have shown that exercise gives rise to images of the future, allowing the mind to think more effectively.

Running also helps the brain become more focused. Running acts as a cleansing ritual, providing a clean slate after exercise. The willpower required to complete long marathons easily translates into everyday life. When you develop a solid nutritional regimen and add exercise to the mix, your body adjusts to work with the energy it is given.

Increase self-esteem

It's no secret that running builds self-esteem. As the body begins to acclimate to running, it develops stronger, leaner muscles. Constant running will undoubtedly change the way the body looks and functions, ultimately leading to greater body satisfaction. Seeing yourself become a fitter version of yourself is the first step in gaining self-esteem.

However, changing the body is not the only reason for increasing self-esteem. In a study conducted by Dr Dorothy L. Schmalz, 197 girls between the ages of 9 and 13 showed a greater increase in self-confidence when competing at higher skills than their counterparts. For ten years they have studied children who answered the question: "Would you rather stay inside and watch TV or play, or would you rather spend time outside to play" (Schmalz, 2007). Those who responded with a desire to spend more time outdoors at age 11 or 13 showed an increase in the level of self-esteem of those who preferred to spend more time indoors.

The study concludes that those who spend more time outdoors generally have a greater increase in self-esteem as they age because they are more active. They receive natural endorphins that help reduce anxiety and depression, preventing the first cases of self-esteem problems. The study also showed a lack of BMI addiction, meaning children who were older and enjoyed spending time outdoors more than indoors showed the same amount of body positivity.

Any aerobic exercise is good for both body and mind, but running is especially beneficial. Running outdoors ensures that the body gets both fresh air and sunlight, two factors that also improve mood. The sense of accomplishment after the run also adds to positive attitudes. Those who do not participate in activities are often less likely to feel secure due to a sense of frustration from lack of effort.

Physical benefits

No list of running benefits would be complete without mentioning the physical benefits that come with running. After all, this is why many people choose to run in the first place.

The race has had a significant history, mainly due to its accessibility. Sports such as disco, boxing and gymnastics have existed for millennia; they can't compare with the past of racing. Humans aren't the fastest runners in the animal kingdom, but we're one of the best endurance running species. Few animals can sustain a steady pace for the distance of a marathon, all thanks to evolution.

Our early ancestors weren't born to run, but over time they developed the ability to survive. The human body contains muscles in the legs that allow us to store energy and then release it in a spring-like explosion that is unique to almost all other creatures except the cheetah (Stipp, 2012). Our bodies also house some of the best heat release mechanisms, which allow us to expel heat through sweating, a feature unique to humans. Due to evolution, our bodies can handle long distance running. We are destined to run.

It may be possible to run long distances, but why should you do it? Well, in addition to pushing yourself to the limit, running affects the body in a positive way. Running affects your body by helping heart health, gaining a slimmer figure, and adding days, weeks, or even years to your life. It is also one of the most popular types of exercise due to its ability to affect the whole body at the same time. Because it is an integral part of our DNA, running provides the body with extraordinary strength and improves the body over time.

Strengthens bones and muscles

Many people believe that running negatively affects the body. The pain experienced by first-time runners and even long-time runners makes it hard to disagree with this statement, especially when you're on the pavement hearing every step. The impact on the joints and bones of constant stress while running is the supporting argument for running that causes osteoporosis, a disease that decreases bone density. Running is often linked to this disease because those who suffer from knee and hip injuries are more likely to get this disease.

However, running itself is responsible for strengthening the joints and cartilage. In a study by Paul T. Williams (2013), he used feedback from nearly 90,000 runners to determine whether osteoporosis was caused by running. Over 50,000 of these participants ran marathons each year, and each was divided into groups to determine if the number of races the runners competed in helped develop osteoporosis. The results, conducted on runners who ran one to five marathons a year, showed no direct correlation with the disease. Of course, some people ran more often than others, but they were not at a greater risk of developing osteoporosis than those who ran less.

Another major cause of osteoporosis is weight. So, instead of showing a direct correlation with osteoporosis, running is a preventative measure. Runners lose weight due to long periods of exercise, reducing their risk. Runners who are not careful about preventing injuries often experience them, so it's extraordinarily important to follow proper stretching techniques.

Running is often known as an open chain exercise. This means that the body experiences stress on contact with the ground. When your feet touch the floor, they make direct contact with a hard surface, putting stress on the bones. This grinding in the body allows blood to flow more easily through the body during exercise. The calcium in the bloodstream is then absorbed into the bones, strengthening them.

Runners can also experience better joint health. Because you build muscle as you run, your joints are cushioned from any impact, generally showing better health than those not exercising. Many people associate arthritis with running because it is a high impact sport, but studies have shown that there is no correlation between running and arthritis. Runners are often advised to include strength training with their regular workouts to build joint strength. The key to maintaining good joint health is taking care of your body. While there are always excuses for not grabbing running shoes, injuries are a major cause of arthritis.

Decreases cravings for unhealthy food

Just as running is extremely helpful in overcoming substance abuse, so it is with unhealthy food cravings. Unhealthy food, while not often seen as an addiction, affects some people more than others in ways similar to drug addiction. Sugars, fats and salts can be addictive over time, and it is often difficult to quit once consuming these foods becomes a lifestyle.

Running can curb your addiction to unhealthy food. Those who ran showed a greater inclination to choose healthy foods after the run than those who chose not to exercise. A study conducted determined how the brain was affected after running. Using males that ran at high speeds for an hour, the scientists performed brain scans while the men looked at images of the food. Those who had been running at a fast pace for an hour exhibited fewer cravings than those who did not. Basically, the mind becomes less interested in unhealthy foods after high intensity exercise. Hunger was suppressed and hormones usually created when hunger showed lower levels.

If you're new to running, you probably haven't experienced the pain of maintaining an unhealthy diet when exercising consistently. It is common to experience an upset stomach when eating too many unhealthy foods during a running program. This alone is a significant reason for many to abandon processed sugars, fats, and salts and base their diets on consuming high-protein protein and vegetables. Not only does the body have more energy when it consumes healthier foods, but it feels better overall.

Allows for better sleep

For those who have exercised consistently in the past, it should come as no surprise that aerobic exercise helps you sleep better. After all, your body starts to wear out after long periods of activity.

We use our bodies much less than we have in the past. The first humans were hunters and gatherers who had to use both strength and endurance to survive in both harsh and lush environments. The body had to hold up as those who gathered food often bent, twisted, and moved during the day. Hunters needed stamina and athletic ability to receive prey. Even as humans evolved, the body continued to work in different functions: agriculture, construction, navigation, to name a few. It was not uncommon to travel all day every day. However, the past few centuries have shown a change in basic bodily function. With machines we can stay in one place and the use of our mind has become a important skill for survival. The human race simply doesn't get the exercise it was used to. Exercise, therefore, is an essential part of daily life, and sleep is better when added to the daily routine. Running, one of the most basic human exercises, is a great place to start.

A study conducted at Northwestern University used a group of adults with insomnia and no exercise records to determine how sleep problems would improve after consistent exercise. The group was split in two, the control group that would not exercise and the group that would. The study ended after 16 weeks, and those who exercised noticed noticeable improvements in their sleep patterns and sleep quality.

According to psychological studies, however, sleep does not improve immediately after running once. It can take weeks or months for the benefits of better sleep to manifest. Many who start their exercise journeys believe they will reap the benefits of sleep aid after just one week. While it might help you moderately, you won't see significant results until you start exercising more consistently. While this may be unfortunate news for some, the study showed there was a correlation over time. The key to good sleep, then, is to stick to an exercise routine.

Since running is also very effective for those with anxiety and depression, you may notice a change in your sleep patterns after a few sessions. Both mental illnesses prevent the mind from turning off, which starts the sleep process. The chemicals released after running allow the body to experience a revival of mood, which will help the mind overcome difficult obstacles.

It helps you to live longer

Perhaps one of the most common benefits of running is the fact that it helps heal a body and allows you to live longer. Many believe that going on the track often and for long periods helps with a long life, but even a little bit can give you a few more years.

Australian researchers studied fourteen studies on the effects of running on nearly a quarter of a million participants. The studies ranged from short (5.5 years) to longer (35 years). Each study marked what happened to the participants after they ran consistently or inconsistently over the study years. Perhaps unsurprisingly, research showed that those who ran more displayed healthier lives than those who ran less. In all, the data "Collective data showed that any amount of stroke was associated with a 30% lower risk of death from heart disease and a 23% lower risk of death from cancer" (Preidt, 2019). Basically, those who practiced a healthier lifestyle through running had a healthier body.

Sure, that doesn't sound like new, but research has also determined health differently. Most research has shown that it doesn't matter how much time you spend running for health benefits as long as it becomes part of your week. The study found that running, one of the most accessible forms of exercise, only took one hour a week to make them healthier.

This shouldn't discourage you from running longer if you can. Studies have also shown that there has been an increase in the health benefits of those who have chosen to run more. Basically, if you want to increase your overall health and the ability to live longer, spend the time running more. Running reduces the risk of hypertension, obesity, type 2 diabetes, and high cholesterol. The more prone you are to having these problems, the more important it is to run consistently.

As racing in many vocations is rapidly drawing to a close, it is imperative that running becomes part of our culture now. Obesity is a common problem and sitting all day and eating unhealthy foods is becoming a daily part of life. To become a healthier nation, many scientists suggest running is the answer. It is easy, accessible and essential to the overall health of the world.

Get into the right mindset

It may seem contradictory, but physical stability really starts in the mind. In order for your body to move, you need the right mindset. Here are some common reasons people give for not running. How many of these have you used yourself?

You don't have enough time

You may be thinking, "I don't have time to run" or "Running isn't the most important thing I have to do today." But you can choose how you spend your time. Ask yourself what is the most important thing you need to do today. What are you dedicating yourself to? How important is your health to you? Keep in mind that of the most effective exercise options, running takes the least amount of time.

You are worried about how you will look

You may also worry about how you will look while running, even worry about looking silly. If you think everyone else running seems silly too, at least you'll be in good company! When you are you you feel good, however, you will not look or feel silly. Likewise, you may not like the prospect of sweating a lot when running. Just remember that sweating is a natural function of the body and you will be happy to have a functioning cooling system.

You don't want to get hurt

If you are afraid of getting hurt while running, read on. when done correctly, running should be neither uncomfortable nor harmful. This book will help you systematically learn to run safely so that you reach a level of tness that results in a healthier lifestyle. Finally, don't worry about being too old to run. This is the mentality of your old life. Start your new life today. Nobody is too old to run.

You don't want to spend the money

Maybe you are concerned that the ride is expensive and has hidden costs. However, running is probably the cheapest form of exercise. Plus, being unhealthy is costly in the long run.

No more excuses: time for the new you

There are always excuses for not doing what you really want to do. You will probably recognize from the previous section the excuses you have made in the past for not rushing. Now is the time to stop making excuses. To prepare to be a runner, you need a new way of thinking about running.

Change your attitude

First, let go of preconceived ideas about stability and running. Recognize and release old negative attitudes. These unhealthy roadblocks are no longer useful to you. You have a choice as to what to think about, so let those negative thoughts go and start over.

Maybe you think you'll never have fun running. Instead, think about the benefits it provides: new friends, improved energy, better mood, weight loss, and a healthier lifestyle. As with most new runners who persevere, you'll likely learn to love running if you give it a chance.

It is best to approach running with an adventurous spirit. When was the last time you tried something new and healthy? Challenge yourself; be a risk taker. If nothing else works to motivate you, think about the phrase Nike made famous: "Just do it!"

Find time to run

Think of running as a non-negotiable daily activity. Do you think if you will brush your teeth every day or not? Your dental hygiene is a non-negotiable part of your routine that you wouldn't think you wouldn't do. This is how you should start thinking about running. It is an activity to be included in your day.

Treat the time spent running as if you have a health appointment with yourself. If you've suffered from a life-threatening illness but through regular treatments you could recover your health, wouldn't you plan your time to go to those dates? Well, running is a lifesaving appointment! It can help prevent a variety of sedentary medical conditions, such as cardiovascular disease and diabetes.

Build a relationship with running

Becoming a runner requires more than a short-term commitment. Add rush to your life as you would to build a long-term relationship: day in and day out. Start slowly, like when two people start dating. Invest the time to get to know yourself as a runner and your relationship with running will grow.

Build a solid relationship with running. You don't start running by running a marathon. Go for short workouts and be proud of what you accomplish. Learn by taking baby steps and your relationship with running (or running / walking) will become an air of love for a lifetime.

Focus on the health benefits of running

Turn your view of health upside down. How much time do you spend looking after your appearance, worrying about clothes, hair, nails and skin? Many people spend more time looking after their outer appearance than their inner health. The truth is, your outward appearance depends on your underlying health. The next time you look in the mirror, take a deeper look at your body. Imagine how running will improve both the appearance and inner health of your body. Which one looks better to you: a new piece of clothing or the way your clothes t after losing 5-15% of your body fat?

Think of your lead time as an investment in your health that produces invaluable returns. With only half an hour a day, you can reap the rewards. You, not other market conditions, control this investment. Regular running is critical to achieving optimal health and at the same time helping protect you from many preventable diseases. Operating costs can be less expensive than you pay for most life insurance policies, and you realize the benefits while you are still alive. "As an emergency doctor, I face my share of stressful days (and nights). I have always found, however, that I feel better, perform better and am actually a more empathic doctor when I work after running. I am convinced of a neuro-hormonal response that takes place in my body and that gives me energy, but at the same time calms me and helps me to focus, even in difficult circumstances. "- Dr. Ben Bobrow, Las Vegas, NV

Talk to other runners

If you ask runners how they feel after including regular exercise in their life, would you expect them to say one of the following?

Running makes me feel lethargic, grumpy and stressed out.

Running makes me feel worse about myself.
Running makes me feel and look terrible in my clothes.
Running makes me fatter.
Running makes my sleep poorer.
The ride got me started smoking and drinking. Running makes my blood pressure go up.

Obviously not! You probably know that people who run regularly say just the opposite. They boast renewed energy, a better outlook on life, a tendency to eat healthier foods, a better quality of sleep, and more. What is it about the race that produces such e ects? It is the fact that running is a form of aerobic exercise. If your friends are already runners, ask them what they like and what they don't like about running. If they are not runners, ask if they would like to be. Recruit one of your non-racing friends to start a running program with you and share experiences while you train.

You will double your pleasure and be able to share your challenges

Aerobic exercise does for the body what no other activity can do due to a crucial process: using oxygen. You take in oxygen all the time just by breathing, of course. But when you run, you take in more oxygen and it is delivered deeper into the body because the heart, lungs and muscles work harder. Circulation increases and with it the supply of oxygen. This is beneficial for your body and makes you feel good.

The body loves the regular bouts of oxygen-rich exercise and adapts to this. The body actually craves a higher aerobic level. Accommodations are training benefits that improve the body's work not only during exercise but also at rest. No wonder exercise makes us feel better.

Chapter 3

WHY RUN?

Many people think running is a futile endeavor. Spend your time and energy just to get back to the same spot you started from. Others think running is boring and unproductive. I know a couple of them who have nothing against playing football and running across the pitch. They have one goal: to catch the ball and score. For them, running around the block makes no sense. Why would anyone want to do this, they ask.

It is true that it can hurt; It is also true that it requires commitment and willpower, yet millions of people around the world do it regularly.

I can't really give you the answer to why people run. Everyone has their own reasons. Why do we do most of the things we do? Why do we paint? Or skiing? Or play video games?

Some run because they are passionate about it. Others like to push themselves. Other people run because they enjoy the ecstatic feeling of setting a new record. The logic cannot really be found on the running side.

And while I can't tell you why your neighbor goes jogging at five in the morning, I know why you should start running and how you can benefit from hitting the streets.

Running can bring many, many benefits to your life that go far beyond the obvious of shedding the extra pounds.

Running helps you lose weight

Let's start with the most obvious reason. As the most effective way to burn calories, running has become the best weight loss tool for those who want to shed stubborn belly fat. Do you know that a 160-pound person can burn over 850 calories with an hour of running?

Running extends the lifespan

It is not only Chinese herbal remedies that have the power to increase the longevity of life; running can help you stay young too. One of the main benefits running brings is that it keeps us young on the inside, warding off disease and supporting muscle tone and strength.

Running prevents diabetes

Hitting the ground can help you keep blood sugar levels in check by burning excess glucose levels and keeping the blood clean. This is the most powerful weapon against some serious and life-threatening diseases such as diabetes.

Running reduces stress levels

There is no better tool for relieving stress than going out for a run. This physical activity can build balanced emotional health and promotes mental clarity. This is why people struggling with mental and mood disorders are advised to follow a regular running routine.

Running keeps the heart healthy

While it may seem like it at this point, running is not an exercise that deprives you of your free time and hurts your legs. It is an activity that elevates blood flow and heart rate which helps to make the heart arteries move more vigorously. This lowers blood pressure, makes your heart more "elastic" and closes the door to strokes and other cardiovascular diseases.

Running increases lung capacity

When you run, your lungs work hard. The harder they work, the more efficient they become. This will not only prevent you from developing breathing problems as you get older, but will also restore lung health if you were a smoker.

Running strengthens the bones

There is no more bone-friendly exercise than running. Running increases bone density and significantly reduces the risk of developing osteoporosis later in life.

But what about the health benefits? What other aspect of your life can benefit from measuring trails?

Gives you your "I" time

Runners know that this exercise is the best for clearing the mind. And who doesn't need it in this fast-paced world? Did you have a cramped day? Pressure at work? Have you spent hours stuck in traffic? Put on your running shoes, put on your headphones, and enjoy being alone with yourself.

It can help you make new friends

Running is definitely one of the best and easiest ways to make new friends. The best part? You don't have to be afraid to look weird as you will meet health-conscious people who share the same goal and inspiration.

Great news for your furry friend

If you are tired of playing ball with your dog, take him out for a double run. This way you both benefit from the activity, plus it will be a lot of fun.

It can save you money

The ride does not require special signups or expensive commissions. The only thing you need to stay fit and healthy is the right clothing and footwear. Oh, and your motivation, of course.

ARE YOU SUITABLE TO BE A RUNNER?

Running is a task that puts pressure on the body and is a bit physically demanding. That said, not everyone can wear sportswear and go for a marathon.

You can't expect to be able to run 3 miles if you spend your free time as a couch potato. Almost everyone can be a runner, but not everyone is ready to immediately adopt running as a lifestyle choice. This modern society tends to encourage abandonment of the musculoskeletal system which makes the inactive excellent candidates for running injuries.

The first thing you need to do before you even think about buying a new pair of running shoes is to take a look at your medical history. Do you suffer from any health conditions that can affect your run? Are you overweight? Are you underweight? Do you have a heart problem? High blood pressure or diabetes?

The best way to see if you can walk the trails is to visit your doctor. He will measure your blood pressure, assess your weight and height, and advise you accordingly.

Remember, if you are overweight and want to take advantage of the run and shed excess fat, you will probably have to keep that thought for a while. If you don't exercise regularly and are obese, chances are that running will only do you more harm than good.

The extra pounds you carry around put a lot of pressure on your joints, which is why it will be extremely difficult to run. What you need to do is slowly increase your daily activities and balance your diet. Your doctor will likely advise you to start with walks that will help you get fitter and eventually allow you to participate in faster, longer runs.

But what if you are not overweight or have any other health problems? How do you know if you are able to run or not? Well, there are three key points that can send you on track: flexibility, endurance, and strength. Let's do a quick test and see where you are with these:

Your flexibility

Lie on the floor with your legs straight, wrap a towel around your left thigh and hold both ends of the towel with your left hand. With the help of the towel, try to lift your left leg (always keeping it straight) towards your chest. Make sure your right leg and hips don't move. Is it possible to reach a 90 degree angle with the left leg?

Otherwise - If you can't reach 90 degrees it doesn't mean you can't run, it's just that you're not flexible enough. To increase your flexibility, make sure you practice that exercise every day, trying to keep your legs in that position for at least 20 seconds.

Your stamina

Walk 2 miles at your normal speed. How long did it take you? Did you do it in 32 minutes or less?

Otherwise - You are not ready to run yet. Start by walking for 15 to 20 minutes a day to improve your physical activity. When you feel ready to take the baby steps, try our walking / running technique.

Your strength

Try holding a plank (which is the push-up part when your body is up) for three sets of thirty seconds. Also, try doing 10 push-ups and 10 squats. Can you do all this?

Otherwise - Know that having strong legs, cores and arms is essential for running. Before you get started with the running program in this book, try to strengthen your muscles a little.

Chapter 4

CHOOSE THE RIGHT EQUIPMENT

What is there to choose? Put on your shorts and your one pair of running shoes that has been collecting dust on your shoe cabinet since college and visit the nearest park, right?

Well, yes, if you want to limp the next few days. Those running shoes and jogging pants you see in sporting goods stores aren't sold to make you the wackiest and coolest runner in the park. In fact, they are essential for providing you with comfort, ensuring safety and improving your running performance.

But how to choose the right racing equipment? Should you just walk into the store and ask if they have those cute Nikes from your size showcase? It's actually not that simple. There is a lot to consider before going to the registry. Here's what you should know before you go shopping for your first running gear.

FOOTWEAR

Shoes are the runner's greatest asset (in addition to excellent physical condition, of course). When times were simpler, shoes were too. You could buy some plimsolls and run on the sidewalks. So what has changed? Are shoe companies promoting fancy running gear just to maximize their profits?

Actually no. People have made a lot of discoveries since a couple of decades ago, and the fact that bad running shoes are the main culprit of running, injuries is one of them. Sure, there's no magical pair of sneakers that will make you the greatest runner in the world, but choosing the one that fits your feet perfectly is the best health insurance. And I'm not just talking about getting the right size.

There is one very important thing you should know before going to the store, and it is called pronation.

Running, of course, forces your feet to make extremely complex and dynamic movements. When you perform these energetic movements, your feet hit the ground with the outside of your heels. First, they roll down and inward as they touch the ground, and finally the heels lift and the balls of the feet push off the ground.

The degree to which your feet roll inward when they meet the ground is called pronation. But not everyone pronounces as they should. Some people tend to supinate.

Supination is the exact opposite of pronation and occurs when the feet roll outward as they hit the ground, not inward. So before you point your finger at what you think are the best running shoes in the store, be sure to determine your running style and see if you are a pronator or supinator.

The wettest

The wet test is the easiest way to find out your degree of pronation. And it is quite simple. Next time you take a shower, spread a sheet of white paper on the floor of the tub.

If your cards are dark and you can see your fingerprints clearly, there is no need for the card. While your feet are still wet, leave a footprint on the paper (the bath mat works well too). Analyze the shape of the footprint. Printing can take one of these three forms:

It can be arched. If your footprint is curved and emphasizes an arch showing mainly the heel and sole of the foot, then you are a supinator. Supinators are less flexible runners. Their bone structure is quite stiff and their feet cannot absorb shock well.

It can be normal. A normal footprint still has a curve, but it also shows the entire foot. This means that you are normal pronator. Normal pronators are neutral runners. They have the least risk of injury.

It can be flat. If your foot is in full contact with the ground and your footprint shows no arch, you tend to overpronate. Overpronators have a very low instep, and when injured, it is usually the calf muscles that suffer.

Your old shoes can also show you your degree of pronation. Grab a pair and check the shoe line. Does the heel show signs of wear on the inside edge or outside edge?

The construction of the shoe

Your running shoes will be your new best friends and, therefore, it is important to know their anatomy. Also, if you don't know how the shoe is built, you may never find the right size.

The last one - The shape of the shoe is the sole of the shoe, the bottom. The last of the shoe is probably the most important factor that needs to be considered.

There are three types of shoes: straight, curved and semi-curved. You can easily check the type of shoe just by looking at the bottom.

Just imagine that there is a straight line running through the center of the shoe. If the imaginary line divides the shoe into two equal halves, the shoe is straight.

If the line is really curved, then it's a curved shoe. The last half curve has a visible but slight curve at the top.

The three types of shapes correspond to the three types of feet. If you overprone and have flat feet, straight shoes are the perfect choice. They will offer you a supportive and firm base that will control your feet 'tendency to overpronate.

If your feet are prone to outward rolling and you are a supinator, you need shoes with good cushioning that offer flexibility to your feet. Curved shoes will do just that. They will support your feet and force them to roll inward, which will help them better absorb the shock of hitting the ground.

Those of you who are neutral runners are in luck because there's really no need to look for special cushioning or an extra stiff base. Semi curved shoes are the perfect choice for your normal feet.

Superior - The upper is the fabric part of the shoe where the laces are located. This part protects the hips and the top of the feet from the toes to the heels. The design and fabric of the upper does not affect the running process much, so you are free to choose according to your preferences.

Midsole- This is the rubber part that is between the last and the top. The midsole has the task of controlling the movements of the feet and preventing, where possible, the inclination of overpronation or supination.

This cushioning material is usually made up of gel, foam, plastic, and some major manufacturers also use air pockets (Think

Nike Air Max) to reduce the weight of the shoe and increase performance.

Inner sole- The inner soles can be easily removed or replaced. They are located inside the shoe and provide extra cushioning and support.

Heel counter- The buttress is what holds the back of our feet. They are made mostly of cardboard and plastic and are there to hold our feet firmly and keep them from going up and down.

Toe Box- The fingertips are also very important. Just like the feet, the toes are also not the same size. When shopping for shoes, it is extremely important to inspect the fingertips well and see if the toes can be moved from the inside or not. The best way to do this is to place your index finger inside the shoe and see if it can fit between the front of the shoe and the longest toe.

A match made in heaven

The best advice I can give you is to visit a running shop to get the most professional service. The people who work there are trained to give you the best choice that matches your foot type and they will do a much better job than when you decide to measure spans yourself.

Most running shoes will serve you perfectly for around 400-500 miles, and that's the only "critical" purchase you'll need to make.

*Keep in mind:*If you are planning to run a race or marathon in the near future, it is best to buy two pairs of shoes. One that you will use for your training and one that will be new to the marathon. Your training shoes can wear out easily and will most likely reduce your performance on the big day.

These are the general tips when it comes to buying running shoes:

Your feet will most likely swell when running, so it's best to try on shoes in the late afternoon as our feet are the largest at that time.

It is common for people to have different sized feet, so it is best for the seller to measure both feet first.

Put on your socks. It is recommended that you wear running socks when trying on shoes. If you don't have any, it's probably wise to purchase a pair before purchasing shoes.

Try on both shoes and go running up and down the store. Okay, you don't actually have to do a circular run, and it may sound strange, but it's really highly recommended to get an idea of whether or not the shoes fit your running activity. Most decent shops will still have a race car to try it out.

The heel must be firmly pressed against the buttress and not be able to slide up and down.

Your running shoes should be half to full size larger than your regular shoes.

In a perfect world, you should be able to find the perfect shoe in the first store you enter. However, this is unlikely to happen. Many people struggle to find the best running shoes. If you are one of them, wait before giving up on your dream of running a marathon. If stores don't offer what your feet are looking for, try insoles. The orthotics are insoles that are custom built to fit your preferences. These can be hard or soft and made from different materials. The insoles inserted inside the shoe repair the specific defects of the shoe and offer your foot excellent support that will improve its performance.

CLOTHING

Nobody says you actually have to have special clothes designed for running to go jogging. However, if you are serious about running and being healthy and want to improve your performance while staying safe, choosing the right clothes to wear can make a huge difference.

First of all, when it comes to running apparel, keep in mind that it's the quality that matters. You don't have to buy 5 running bras. It is a far better option to have a specially designed one and wash it daily, rather than having a quantity that lacks quality.

Running clothing, just like any other clothing, is mostly determined by the weather outside. If that's how you dress less. If not, the extra levels are the best. You're thinking, okay, but what to wear? The most important question is what not to wear. And I have only one answer to this question: cotton. That new cotton shirt can be great for going out for a drink, but if you wear it to run, it'll keep you in bed for days. Yes, cotton clothes make you catch a cold easily. Such as? Cotton doesn't dry that easily. When it gets wet, it stays wet for many hours. You don't go out wearing wet clothes, do you? Likewise, you shouldn't run in wet clothes. This will not only make your running experience super uncomfortable, it will also be dangerous.

Now, back to the "what to wear" question. As I said, depending on the weather, you can wear clothing designed for running: shirts, tights, shorts, pants, bras, jackets and vests. In hot weather, your running clothes should protect you from the heat and keep you cool. In cold weather, running clothes will keep you warm, but make sure you are not hot, as you will warm up once you start running and sweating.

When looking to buy running clothes, there are a couple of factors you need to consider:

Quick drying - The perfect running clothing needs to be able to absorb sweat quickly, keep you dry and protected from the cold. *Moisture Absorption* - The breathable fabric quickly wicks sweat away from the skin and keeps you dry.

Thumb holes- Many long sleeve running clothes have thumb holes that will keep your hands warm. You can skip the gloves if your thumb jacket completely covers your hands.

Sun protection - Always choose clothing with a high degree of UPF that will protect you from the sun's UVA and UVB rays.

Compression - Compression running clothes provide a comfortable fit and keep you comfortable.

Inner lining - When shopping for shorts, it is recommended that you purchase those that have an inner lining that can act as underwear and decrease drag.

Mesh air vents- Buy only tops with mesh panels. This can keep the hips, armpits, back, and other areas of the body easily warmed up and cool.

The fabric

The fabric of your running clothes is not only important but crucial. Before purchasing the pants by design, check the label and see if it is made of "technical" clothing. The technical fabric is light, breathable, anti-itch and, above all, it will keep the skin dry:

Merino wool - Besides that, it contains all the features mentioned above, merino wool is also antimicrobial which will keep the smell away. It is the best fabric for regulating body temperature which means it will keep you cool when it is hot and keep you warm when the temperature drops.

Polyester - Polyester is great for keeping moisture away from the skin, improving your running performance.

Nylon - Whether used alone or mixed with other quick-drying fabrics, nylon is a great breathable fabric that is extremely durable.

*IMPORTANT:*Have you ever wondered why running shoes and clothes have such bright and vivid colors? It's to keep you safe on the road. Running in the middle of the day isn't always an option. Sometimes, when the days get shorter or your schedule doesn't allow it, you'll find yourself hitting the ground at night. You have to stay a moment in those moments. Bright vests, jackets and dresses with reflective stripes will make you see even when the streets aren't well lit.

OTHER EQUIPMENT

You don't really have to spend half your salary on fancy gadgets to be a great runner. And while running gear other than the right pair of shoes and comfortable, breathable clothing may not be essential, there are some goodies your running can really benefit from:

> *Heart Monitor* - If your doctor thinks it might be wise for you to monitor your heart rate, then the heart rate monitor is something you should always have with you when you run. It's amazing advice that will tell you when it's time to slow down, even if your legs don't want to listen. This is great for those who tend to over train and need an alarming sound to stop them.
>
> *Sun glasses*- Don't let the scorching red sun send you home earlier and put an end to your morning routine. But peeking through shouldn't be an option

either. Make sure you have a nice pair of running shoes with you when you run. There is no need to buy a high-tech pair that will hurt your heart if you leave them on a bench somewhere. However, make sure that the sunglasses you choose offer you 100% ultraviolet protection.

Clock - What better way to see how long you've been running than the old-fashioned wrist check? The trail isn't exactly the right place for your Rolex, but buying an affordable running watch that has all the features you need will be a great investment.

Fresh towels- Buy a cool towel, dry it and snap it a few times and you will have the perfect relief from the high summer temperatures. These towels won't make you jealously chill, but they are just what can cool you when the sun starts burning your skin.

A folding belt - If your clothes don't have pockets, a Flip Belt is the perfect solution for storing items. The Flip Belt is a belt in which you can store your ID, keys and phone. You can lock everything by simply flipping the belt over.

Yaktrax - Who says you have to go to the gym when it's snowing outside? Who says the treadmill is the only option when the streets are snowy and icy? Just like you put those chains on the wheels of a car, the same way you put the yaktrax on your running shoes. Yaktrax are super convenient, easily attached, and will give you a great grip that will keep you from falling onto your butt.

BEFORE YOU LACE YOUR RUNNING SHOES

Running is one of those things that everyone wants to be good at, but most people don't know how. Be honest and answer this. Have you ever tried to run only to give up 5 minutes later? I know a couple of them who bought the most expensive racing equipment and gave up the dream of racing the next day. Is the lack of determination the problem? Or is running so damn boring? What makes people fear the thought of jogging in the mornings?

If you want to be a runner but don't want to fall into one of the many traps this modern world will most likely throw at you, read on to see how not to fail in running.

Time, not miles. The first reason people fail is because they are easily disappointed. They set the bar too high and when they can't reach the desired goal, they throw their running shoes out the window. Don't start your running journey by running in miles, but in minutes. It is much more productive to try running 15 minutes than 3 miles. Don't measure distance, but try to increase the time you run, a little bit every day.

Have a goal. No matter how small, having a goal to achieve is the best motivational indicator. For example, let's say your goal is to be able to run 5 miles without stopping. Of course, you can't do this after 2 days of being a novice runner. The best way is to try to split the 5 mile goal into other smaller goals. In order to run 5 miles, you will need improved fitness and much better physical condition. So, you may want to make eating right, exercising and running for x minutes each day, your sub-goals.

Keep a diary. Keeping a log and making it easier for yourself to view your running progress is the perfect tool to keep you motivated. Being able to see how your performance progresses each day will keep you on track and give you the boost to do even better.

Find a friend. Although running is considered a solitary sport, quitting is usually easier for those beginners who tackle this challenging task on their own. Instead, why not find a fitness-conscious friend and invite them to start this journey together? This way you can keep each other motivated and besides, it's a lot more fun.

Get some rest. Rest days are just as important as training days. It's your time to recharge your batteries and charge yourself up with extra energy that can boost your running performance. Pushing yourself too hard will not only exhaust you, it can also hurt you. Don't be drastic, but be patient. If you want it badly, you can run a marathon. If it's possible for Oprah, it's possible for you too.

WALK TO RUN

Most of us can easily walk a couple of miles before fatigue sets in. Walking is natural for us as we are designed so that we can do it efficiently for a couple of hours. Running, on the other hand, puts us under more pressure, simply because it requires more work. In order to run, you need to lift your feet and body off the ground and then land on it again. And you have to do it again and again. This means that during the running process, your body will constantly receive the shock of landing. For those who are not in decent physical condition, this process will result in fatigue, aches, body aches or even some more serious injuries.

But just because you've been a couch potato all your life doesn't mean you have to injure yourself to become a fit runner. There is a safe method that allows beginners to improve their form so they can start running the right way and keep those injuries at bay. This is the walk / run method.

The walk / run method, as the name suggests, is a combination of running and walking. It is perfect for beginner runners who want to decrease fatigue and become able to run without having to stop for a break every 15 seconds. And although when it comes to starting a run it may seem like something designed for a third level, the walking / running technique can really make a difference:

It can be a great motivator in the beginning, which is extremely important It can help you control fatigue and exhaustion which can be of great help later on as it can prevent injuries   It can train you to endure long runs and finish your races

Do you know that many experienced runners also combine walking and running? They say it relieves pressure on the muscles, which is great for eliminating injuries and for mileage endurance.

Now that we've made it clear that the walk / run method won't embarrass you once you join the experienced runners in the park, let's see how you can actually start this workout.

First of all, know that running is nothing like learning to ride a bike. You can't master it in one day. You will need to slowly develop your condition and pace, and this will take some time. Or 8 weeks to be precise. I highly recommend doing the walking / running style for a full 8 weeks before you start setting higher goals and start pushing yourself. And here's how you can get started:

Warm up. Before you start hammering, you must first warm up with a 5-minute walk. Never start running the moment you leave the house. Instead, warm up your muscles with a short walk.

Get the right starting ratio. This is a very simple method; the only thing you need to do is get the 1: 6 ratio right the first week. This means that after 1 minute of jogging, you should be walking for 6 minutes. For example, if you decide you can run for 3 minutes, you should walk for 18 minutes before you start running again.

Walk before you get tired. The biggest mistake that inexperienced runners make is that they run until they lose their breath completely. Once you are exhausted, it will take a lot longer for your muscles to recover and you will likely stop running. By slowing down and switching to a walk before you get too tired, your muscles will recover quickly and you can cover more distance and time.

Walk right. Walk slowly, but do it with a strong, short step. Make sure you don't take it slow, but keep your arms pumped so you can keep your heart rate high so you can easily get back to running.

Increase gradually. Over time, you should gradually decrease your walking time and increase your jogging time.

If you want to improve your condition and become able to run for 30 minutes continuously, this 8 week walking / running program will help you achieve just that:

Week 1 - Start walking for five minutes to warm up. Jog for one minute, then go back to walking and walking for 6 minutes. Repeat three times. It is recommended that you run for three sessions this first week.

Week 2- Warm up by walking for five minutes. Run for 2 minutes, then walk for five. Repeat four times. Do three running sessions this week.

Week 3- Again, start walking for 5 minutes. Switch to running and jogging for 4 minutes and slow down by walking for 2. Repeat four times. Do four running sessions this week.

Week 4 - After walking for five minutes, run for 5 and walk for 2 minutes. Repeat 4 times. This session is expected to be done three times this week.

Week 5 - After warming up, run for 8 minutes and walk for two. Repeat four times. Do three sessions this week.

Week 6- Warm up, jog for nine minutes and walk for two. Repeat three times and this week also do three running sessions.

Week 7 - Walk for one minute and run for 11. Repeat three times and do three weekly running sessions.

Week 8 - Try walking for five minutes, run for 20, and finish your workout by walking for five minutes again. Increase your running time each day so that by the end of this week you can run for 30 minutes non-stop.

After this, you will be able to run 30 minutes non-stop without getting tired. You should do this three times a week.

Chapter 5
TO START

Those of you who think running is easy aren't that far from the truth. You can really just put on your running shoes, put your headphones on and hit the road. It can be that simple. However, when you're still not familiar with the good and bad things that can happen after hitting the sidewalks, you may want to keep that extra energy and make sure you're fully prepared for this challenging process first.

To get you on the right track, this chapter will explain everything you need to know before starting your long non-stop runs. From where to start running to how to cool off after a good run, let this chapter be the guide that will help you reach your running goals.

WHERE TO RUN?

Yes, you can run anywhere, be it the sidewalk in your neighborhood, the sand on the beach or that hill up the mountain. Your feet will hit the same no matter what terrain you choose to put under them. So what's the problem with choosing the right surface? While your feet may be fine with landing on hard and soft surfaces, your body is a bit more demanding. Evenness of the surface is also very important and in many situations it is the main cause for injuries to occur. The pressure your body receives when your feet hit uneven ground indicates the possibility of injury. But is there a better surface that will be your body's best friend and boost your running performance? Many say there is, however, when you are just starting to run, I would say an ideal surface for you would be forest ground stuffed with pine needles. But since only a few of us actually have the privilege of having this ideal surface nearby, the rest of us have to work with what our surroundings offer.

Experts say the key to success is variety, which means choosing to mix the terrain you run on is key to your healthy performance. Of course I don't mean to literally mix them up, but just to avoid running a single trail every day.

Each running surface comes with a list of pros and cons, and to determine when to walk which of these routes, you need to know how and when your body can benefit from them.

Grass. If there is no forest nearby, there is no need to sprinkle pine needles on the road to avoid injury, grass will do just fine. The herb also has a low impact on the body and is therefore recommended for beginners. I can understand why flooring may seem like a more affordable option to you, but keep in mind that this is the best surface to avoid injury at this early stage. Many studies have concluded that weed is the friendliest surface for our body because it lowers the pressure on muscles, tissues and bones.

But weed can be tricky. Know that running in the park can be a bit stressful due to all the distractions like dogs and walkers. Also, you need to be more careful when running on grass and watch out for those hidden holes and rocks that can cause another type of injury.

Dirty. Dirt roads are ranked as the second best surface for running due to their combination of hardness and flexibility, which can be great for those runners who have suffered an impact injury in the past.

However, just like grass surfaces, dirt can be uneven too, so be careful with your steps to avoid injuring your ankles.

Sand. The sand looks great simply because it is soft and the risk of suffering an impact injury is minimal. A run on the beach can also be more relaxing, not only for the environment but also for the low pressure this surface exerts on the muscles.

But the sand isn't as big as it looks. The softness of the sand makes it a rather unstable surface that screams ankle injuries. Running on sand requires a lot of strength as it is difficult to get a good grip. For beginners, it is recommended to avoid these sand-related accidents. If, on the other hand, you particularly love running on the beach, do it on wet sand because it is a very safe surface.

Asphalt. If your goal is to train for a race, at some point (usually after "dominating" the grass), your feet must meet the asphalt to prepare you, as most races take place on the road. The asphalt lowers heel tension and has proven to be a pretty great running surface as well.

Keep in mind that running on the street is not safe. Make sure you wear bright colors with reflective stripes that will get you noticed. Also, lose your headphones in order to increase your awareness and reduce danger.

Concrete. Those of you who live in big cities will find running on sidewalks to be the safest and most affordable option. However, it is also the worst. Know that concrete is one of the hardest surfaces and can, therefore, increase stress on the joints and muscles. While good shoes with adequate cushioning can help, try to limit the running time you spend on the sidewalks.

Tapis Roulant. First of all, know that running the same distance on the treadmill and on a real surface is not the same thing. The treadmills also pull you while you run, which makes the whole process easier and allows you to run long distances. Driving the same mileage on asphalt or grass will be more complicated.

Now, the treadmill as a running surface is great if you have suffered an injury or want to reduce stress on your muscles. However, not being able to observe your surroundings as you pass them can be boring and quite daunting.

Hills. Although the climbs are really determined by the area itself, beginners should try to avoid running up and down hills and climbs whenever possible. Running uphill requires excellent physical condition and running strength, which you lack in this initial phase. Running down a hill may seem like a better choice as it can pick up the pace. However, this is only in the short term, as downhill slopes put too much stress on the joints.

So which one to choose? Start with grass, avoid hills where possible, then mix other surfaces. Having a running course is great, but always running on the same surface, not so much.

HEATING TECHNIQUES

"But I'm not training for a marathon." It doesn't matter if you run to prepare for the upcoming marathon, if you do it for fun or if you use running as a tool to relieve stress. Warming up before you start running is essential if you want to stay in good shape and prevent injuries.

The biggest mistake beginners make when running is that they skip the warm-up part altogether, thinking it's an unnecessary waste of energy that could possibly cover an extra mile. This is not only wrong, but absurd. Warm-up techniques are used to prepare legs and muscles to endure long distances, not to absorb energy and contribute to exhaustion.

And while we said that walking before a run is a great way to warm up tissues and prepare your legs for running, it's just not enough. Sure, the walking / running technique doesn't really require any special strength or training, but if you want to make running an important addition to your lifestyle, making sure you maintain your fitness and peak performance is key.

Make sure you set aside 10 minutes to warm up before hitting the ground. This will awaken your central nervous system, raise your body temperature, increase your heart and breathing rate, and prepare your whole body for the effort of running.

Won't a simple stretch fit? It is important to remember that for many years, warming up and stretching have been terms used interchangeably. Now that we know better, we not only know that they mean two different things, but we also know that basic and static 30-second stretching is just the opposite of beneficial, as it has been linked to injury.

Dynamic stretching, on the other hand, loosens muscles and improves leg movement:

Toe Walk. This simple exercise will build strength around the ankles and activate the muscles in the shin, calf and feet.

Stand with your spine straight and your shoulders back hip-width apart.

Lift your heels off the ground, keeping your balance on the balls.

Take a step forward with your right foot as you extend onto your toes.

Balance as you swing your left arm.

Repeat with your left foot and right hand and keep walking that way.

Heel Walk. This exercise will reduce heel tension, as well as activate the muscles in the lower leg and ankles.

Assume the same posture as in the previous exercise. Straight and with legs hip-width apart.

Lift your toes off the ground, keeping your balance on your heels.

Step forward with your right foot, keeping your toes pointing up.

Balance as you swing your left arm.

Repeat with your right foot and continue walking on your heels.

Inchworm Walk. This is a slightly more challenging exercise that can mobilize not only the leg muscles but also the shoulders and lower back.

> Get into a push-up position, which means your hands should be on the floor and under your shoulders, your arms and spine straight, your feet hip-width apart, and your balance on your toes.
>
> Now try to walk with your feet towards your hands, which means your body should be bent at the hips.
>
> Hold that position, then slowly bring your feet back to the initial flexion step. To repeat.

Walk with the knee straight. This will activate the calf muscles and mobilize your body.

Stand straight and keep your legs hip-width apart.

Extend your left arm in front of you, parallel to the floor.

Lift your right leg and bring it closer to you. Ideally, the leg should touch the left arm, but if you can't, lift it as high as possible.

Hold this position briefly, then step with your right leg.

Repeat with the other side and keep walking like this.

Hip exercise. Mobility of the hips is essential for proper running performance. This exercise will open your hips and make them more flexible.

Stand straight with your feet hip-width apart.

Lift your right leg. With your left hand, grab your right leg at the ankle.

Grab the knee with your right hand.

Slowly lift your leg towards your chest.

Hold that position, then release and repeat with the other side.

Scorpion Stretch. This exercise is perfect for mobilizing the core and improving the flexibility of your body, essential for proper performance.

Lie on the floor (preferably on a mat) with your face down.

Stretch your arms to form a 90 degree angle with your body and keep your palms flat on the floor.

Slowly, lift your right hip off the floor.

Now, gently bring your right foot over your back as if you are trying to reach for your left hand. Your back should be bent and your right knee bent.

Hold this position briefly.

Repeat with the other side.

Spiderman. This exercise works on both legs and also improves hip flexibility.

Get into a knee flex position, which means that your knees should be on the ground and your hands should also be.

Place the right foot near the outside of the left hand, keeping the knee bent 90 degrees and level with the armpit.

Now, reach forward with your left hand, step forward and extend your left foot.

Repeat with the other side.

Superman. This simple exercise will increase running performance and endurance by increasing the stability of the knees, ankles and hips.

Stand straight and keep your feet hip-width apart.

Extend your right hand in front of you, parallel to the floor. The palm should be facing down.

Lift your right leg off the floor and stretch it until it is parallel to the floor.

Bend your upper body and left knee for stability.

Extend your right arm more.

Hold this position briefly. Repeat on the other side.

Repeat these exercises for 10 minutes and you are good to go.

Chapter 6

COOLING TECHNIQUES

Just like warming up, cooling your muscles after a run is just as important. By doing it right, you can prevent pain, injury, and gradually reduce your elevated heart rate. And while basic and static stretches can help you cool off (not warm up like people thought), there are also other more muscle-oriented techniques that will help you properly congratulate yourself on completing a challenging workout.

Downward Dog. This stretch will strengthen the calf and core muscles and can prevent Achilles tendon injury.

Place your knees and hands on the floor, keeping your back parallel to the floor and your knees just below your hips.

Raise your knees and lower your heels.

Push your hips up, so that your body has a V shape.

Hold this position briefly, then return to the first step. To repeat.

Adductor stretching. This exercise works the adductor muscles of the hips and thighs.

Stand straight and keep your feet hip-width apart.

Bend the left leg so that the knee reaches over the left foot.

Your right leg should be extended. Repeat on the other side.

Lateral rotation. This stretch relaxes the front of the body from the stress of running.

Lie on your back with your hand on a folded towel and keep your arms at your sides.

Place a foam roller on the right side, bend the left knee and place it on the roller.

Also bend your right leg and let it turn in the direction of rotation. You can extend the stretch by reaching your left arm in the opposite direction (behind you).

Go back to the first step and repeat on the other side.

Hip flexor stretch. This simple exercise can prevent pelvic imbalances.

Kneel on your left knee with your toes tucked under.

Place your right foot in front of you, keeping your right knee at a 90 degree angle.

Put your hands on your hips.

Bend forward and place your weight on your right leg, bending your knee over your right foot.

Hold briefly, then repeat on the other side.

Brettzel. This exercise is great for improving chest mobility.

Lie on your right side and rest your head on a folded towel.

Pull your left knee towards your chest and hold it with your right hand.

Bring your right foot back so that you can grab it with your left hand. Hold briefly, go back to the start and repeat on the other side.

Stretching of the hamstrings. This simple stretch will loosen the hamstrings after a workout and prevent injuries.

Lie on your back on the floor keeping your legs straight and your arms at your sides.

Lift your right leg keeping your toes parallel to your body.

Grab it with your hands and gently pull it back to slightly extend the stretch.

Go back to the first step and repeat on the other side.

THE PERFECT SHAPE

Running is not just putting one foot in front of the other. To project maximum energy with minimum pressure, you must learn to assume the right posture and running form.

When thinking about the right way to run, people mainly focus on their feet and their movements. But you'd be surprised to know that even though running is done with the feet, they actually only play a small part of what we call a great form of running. Whether your feet will hit the ground in the right way or whether they will strain your muscles, believe it or not, depends on your whole body.

Here's detailed information on how to get into perfect shape, reduce muscle stress and improve your condition. Don't feel overwhelmed if you can't perform all of these tips. They are not there to teach you to run, but to run better. Only with regular practice can you adopt each of them and start your workout right.

Boss. Your head plays a key role in how you run and its alignment is critical to your performance. When running, your head should be held high and your gaze directed straight ahead. Avoid looking at your feet to keep your neck, head, and spine straight and aligned for proper shape. Make sure you don't stick your chin out too.

Shoulders. Keep your shoulders wide and low. They should be square and kept level. As your run progresses and you get more tired, you will most likely notice that your shoulders will rise. When this happens, simply shake them to relax them. Try not to swing them too much from side to side.

Arms. Movement of the arms is the key factor in running. By moving your arms, you get the push to push yourself forward, as well as push yourself faster. It is best to keep the arms at a 90 degree angle and move them in the rhythm of the legs. They have to swing, just remember not to swing them on your body. Keep the swing back and forth, but close to your body.

Torso. You have to keep yourself tall and straight at all times. Of course I don't mean to run like a robot; it is natural to lean forward slightly. However, make sure you don't bend over or lean back. Keeping your shoulders in the right position and relaxed should be enough to keep your torso in the right position. Just remember not to twist it from side to side, but run chest high to allow for full lung capacity.

Hands. You should never run with closed fists. Instead, keep your hands relaxed and well structured. Your fingers should touch lightly. If you keep them tense and tight, that tension will be transferred to the rest of your body and weigh down your heart. Just imagine that you are holding a French fries in your hand and you don't want to break it to make sure your hands are not strained.

Hips. The hips are probably the easiest to place in the right way because it's simple. If you keep your shoulders and torso straight, your hips will have no choice but to follow and join in the perfect alignment. Make sure they are facing forward and not leaning forward as this will ruin your entire shape.

Legs. When learning to run correctly, it is natural for beginners to lengthen their stride and lift their knees higher so they can run faster. However, long-distance and experienced runners know that keeping the knees down and short strides is much more productive because that way energy can be preserved. Instead, they increase the turnover of their feet. You should make sure your feet land below your knees, not in front of you. This will keep the steps short and the impact on the knees minimized.

Ankles. While it may seem like they don't move, your ankles should actually roll inward as you run. This will allow you to push yourself forward correctly. If your ankles are too stiff, try some dynamic stretch to loosen your calf muscles.

Feet. Make sure you don't hit with each impact. Instead, land softly and lightly. You should land between your midpoint and heel and rotate your feet forward as you take off. Your feet shouldn't land flat or loud. Running should be light and quiet.

BREATHE CORRECTLY

Breathing is one of the biggest obstacles when it comes to running efficiently. Almost all beginners have struggled with shortness of breath. Ask any experienced runner and you'll get the same answer: when they started, they also experienced the loud snort and snort.

We are trained to breathe from our chest. After all, we do it every second of every day. But this is simply not enough to provide all of our muscles with the necessary amount of oxygen while running. That's when stitches and side pains come.

The way we regulate breathing while running is fundamental to our energy and can, in fact, have a profound impact on all performance. If you want to be a better runner and run a long mileage, you can't do it without the proper breathing method.

Breathe from the belly. Try not to breathe from the chest but from the diaphragm, or as we like to call it, from the belly. Make sure your belly moves up and down with every breath you take.

Breath deeply. Your lungs are small and cannot provide you with enough air to pack all the muscles while you run alone. This is where deep breathing comes in handy. Deep breathing helps you draw more oxygen into your body. When we breathe deeply, the diaphragm is pressed, which causes the lungs and abdomen to expand and fill our lungs with more oxygen. Deep breathing is essential while running because it prevents nausea and fatigue.

Find your breathing pattern. It is really helpful to try to coordinate the breaths you take with your steps. If this seems like an impossible thing to do, you are probably running too fast. Slow down to match your steps with your breath. If you run at a medium pace, try to take a deep breath and hold your breath for three or four steps. Then exhale for the same number of steps. For an intense run, your breathing will also increase to keep up with the pace. When you run hard, one breath for every two steps you take feels right.

Mouth or nose? Do a quick online research on proper breathing techniques for runners and you will find yourself confused by the contradictory advice. Some say you breathe through your nose; others claim that your mouth will help you inhale more oxygen. But which is the best? How do you know which breathing method is best? Well, here's the answer. Breathing through the nostrils allows you to inhale a small amount of air which, unfortunately, is not enough to satisfy the large oxygen demand required by the muscles. Think about blowing a balloon with your nose. Here's how efficient nasal breathing can be while breathing.

This leads us to breathe through the mouth. It is true that inhaling through the mouth will allow for a more consistent flow of oxygen through your body. However, there are many things that are not good about breathing through your mouth while running. Most importantly, when temperatures drop, breathing through the mouth can negatively impact running performance. We all know that fresh air is dry and breathing through your mouth will only give you asthma-like symptoms like wheezing, which your lungs won't like. These symptoms can significantly reduce your energy and ruin your performance.

So what should you do? The best approach is to train both mouth and nose breathing, and most importantly, learn how to do it at the same time. This will significantly increase airflow and provide you with enough oxygen to keep your muscles trained. For spicy weather you can put something on your mouth (like a bandana), which will help keep the moisture out by trapping moisture from your breath.

Practice your breathing. Just as you practice and train to strengthen muscles so that you can improve your performance, so you can train to strengthen your lungs and breathe better:

Sit down and put your hand on your stomach. Take a deep breath and count to 4 every time you exhale or inhale. Check with your hand to see if the belly moves. If it isn't, it means you're not breathing deeply enough.

Go swimming. If you are having a hard time matching your steps with your deep breaths, perhaps swimming can help. Apart from that, it is also a great exercise for the muscles which will help make you a better runner, swimming also puts an emphasis on proper breathing which is yet another way your performance can benefit.

Put your cigarette down. It probably goes without saying, but smokers aren't great runners. Smoking can seriously ruin your running process by damaging your lungs.

Chapter 7: Types of Executions

What is really working? Is jogging different? What are 5k, half marie, fartlek and LSD?

Yes, runners have unique jargon, just like doctors and lawyers have theirs. If you want to be a bona fide runner, it is imperative that you learn the language spoken by the runners. No problem though; there are just a few technical terms to know. And even if you don't learn them right away in this book, you will learn them when you actually start training for a competition. For example, LSDs and timed runs are part of many training programs. You will do them, especially when you train for longer distances like 21k and 42k (referring to a 21km race and a 42km race respectively).

First of all, let's define running and try to differentiate it from jogging. Running means moving forward and covering distance by moving your legs quickly at a faster pace than when walking. It's something we instinctively know how to do, with no need for instructions ... Running coaches recommend a "correct" form of running. Apparently, some people function incorrectly and need to be educated on how to do it correctly. We will get to that in more detail in later chapters. Let's assume for the moment that you can run, that everyone can run.

Jogging is slow. Some people think it is a "trotting". It works at a slow pace, just a little faster than walking. A word of caution though: don't make the mistake of calling a runner a jogger. For some reason, runners in general don't like being called joggers. Perhaps because when they are called jogging, it implies that they run slowly.

There are no officially recognized speeds for running and jogging, but according to some coaches, the demarcation is at 9 miles per hour. Going slower than this is jogging; moving faster than this is running.

Another distinction between running and jogging is that everyone can jog, regardless of age and health condition, but not everyone can run. Presumably, older people and people with health problems can jog, but not everyone can run.

Furthermore, runners and joggers are both motivated by health reasons; they both started the sport to lose weight or to get stronger and healthier. But joggers, presumably, often do it for social interaction as well. The runners, meanwhile, run to prepare for some big race, while the runners don't have that reason.

A "run" is any running session. It can last up to 15 minutes, or it can last up to 24 hours or more in the case of ultra-marathons (or "ultras" for short). A run can be performed alone or together with other runners.

A "race" is a race with a specific distance and course and with registered (paying) participants. It is officiated by a race director and his team. Along the way there are services for runners, the most essential of which are water / food and emergency medical assistance. A race has a specific gun start (start time), a start line (where all runners start running) and a finish line (where they finish).

Training courses

A training run is a run designed to prepare the runner for a specific race distance. It can be done alone or as part of a group. Many training runs make up a "training program," a whole program that typically spans several months to train a runner for a specific race.

There are eight types of training runs. Novice runners don't have to do all of this in their training programs. But it's good to be familiar with all of these types to start your running training.

1. Basic Running: This is done by running a short or medium distance at your "natural pace". While running, you should be comfortable enough, not panting from exertion, but not too relaxed like when walking. This type of running makes up the bulk of a training program. It is meant to be done frequently to get good mileage

basic, i.e. sufficient to make running a habit and to improve the endurance and aerobic capacity of running. Typically, a weekly program consists of two or three basic runs. An example of a basic run, as you can see in a training program, is: 10km at natural / easy pace.

2 TheLong Run - Alongside the base run, this is perhaps the most important run of the week for all types of runners (beginner, intermediate and advanced). It is also called "long, slow distance" (LSD) because it covers a relatively long distance and is done slowly. (If running fast, the runner may not be able to cover the entire

long distance.) In general, any run longer than 1.5 hours is LSD. The distance can be more than 15 or 16 km. Eventually, the runner feels moderately to severely tired. The long run is meant to increase endurance.

3. The Timed Run (or Threshold) - This is perhaps the most difficult of all types of training runs. It is performed at the "lactate threshold level," which is the fastest pace a runner can sustain for about 20 to 30 minutes. The purpose of a timed run is to increase speed. Examples are: 2km of easy jogging as a warm-up, followed by 5km of threshold pace, and finally 2km of easy jogging to cool off. Typically, a runner only runs one timed run in a week.

4. The Interval Run - This run is also called "intervals" because it consists of alternating intervals of slow and fast running. It can also consist of slow runs and walks to allow the runner to recover from fast intervals. The purpose of interval running is to increase speed and develop resistance to fatigue. This is best done on a track where there are segment markers for distances.

Here is an example of an interval session:

> Warm-up: 1km of easy jogging
>
> 5 x 1km at a 5km race pace with 400m walk / jogging recovery Cool down: 1km of easy jogging

The central element refers to the actual intervals. It means that the runner would have to do five intervals, each consisting of 1km of running at the same speed as they would run a 5km race, followed by 400m of walking or jogging to recover.

5 The progression run - This is a moderately demanding run in which the runner starts at his natural (easy) pace and midway through the run (or any time thereafter), moves up to a faster pace and maintains it until the end. In terms of difficulty, progression is more difficult than the base run, but easier than time and interval. Here are two examples:

8 km at natural pace, followed by 2 km at marathon pace and finally 2 km at 10k race pace

5 km at natural pace and 5 km at 5k race pace

The idea is to run slowly and easily in the beginning and gradually increase the pace to the finish.

6. Hill Repeats - These are short, high intensity uphill runs repeated many times. The runner constantly runs uphill, resumes downhill and then repeats the same thing a set number of times (or as often as he can). The ideal hill has a 4 to 6 percent incline, while

steeper inclines provide a more intense workout that increases aerobic power and endurance to fatigue. Uphill repetitions are attempted after the runner has established a comfortable mileage base, that is, after running regularly for a good number of weeks. An example of uphill repetitions is:

> 3km of easy jogging (as a warm-up), 10 reps of 1-minute uphill at intense effort with a 3-minute recovery jog between reps, and 3km of easy jogging (as a cool-down)

7. The Fartlek - Swedish for "game of speed", a fartlek is a race in which the pace is varied throughout, alternating fast and slow segments. Unlike

intervals and progression runs, fartlek is not structured; the runner accelerates and slows down as he pleases, depending on how he feels and perhaps also on the terrain on which he runs. It must, however, include short, fast segments in the run to get the desired benefit from the fartlek.

8 Recovery Run: This is perhaps the simplest of all races. It is done at an easy pace, usually with no target distance or duration. Its purpose is to allow the legs to recover after a competition or intense workout. And oftendone the next day after a difficult run, but can also be done within 8-12 hours after that run. Coaches believe that doing this run accelerates a

person's recovery after the race. It's better than just resting your legs or taking a break from running the day after a strenuous run.

And that completes our list of training paths. Are you surprised how varied the ride can be? You can try to do as many of these runs as you feel comfortable with, bearing in mind that you also need to have a day or two off between these runs. Doing different types of running will likely reduce or eliminate the boredom with running that many beginners experience. Plus, it ensures your improvement in all aspects of running, including speed, aerobic capacity and endurance. Understand that if you were to engage in only one type of running, such as basic running, you would most likely not develop much in terms of speed and fatigue endurance, even if you would improve in endurance and aerobic capacity. So have a mixed combination of rides, within reasonable limits. As mentioned,

Running races and events

Why sign up for a race when you can run alone without having to pay for it? It is true that many runners do not participate regularly in races, preferring instead to run recreationally alone or with their friends.

But it is very difficult to find a runner who has never participated in a race.

When you have been running for some time, you will feel compelled to enter a race to test your progress or to see if you can conquer the race distance. A race is also a great motivation to keep you in training week after week. If there isn't a race you are preparing for, you may feel discouraged or bored running and then slowing down.

Participating in a race is a very rewarding experience that every runner should try. The immense sense of accomplishment and thrill you get when you cross the finish line, especially in the first race, is simply incredible. You also get an official finisher medal and certificate, which are tangible proof of your running achievements that you can hang on a wall at home. And no less important is that rare, bubbly, adrenaline-pumping atmosphere and the friendly yet competitive camaraderie with fellow runners that you can only immerse yourself in at an official racing event.

Finally, many races donate to charities and noble causes, so joining one is very well spent indeed.

Below are the types of races you can start training for and join soon.

3k, 5k and fun rides

There are short races ideal for beginners. As the name suggests, a 3k is a 3km run and a 5k is a 5km run. Many experienced runners also like to join these, especially the 5k, to test their speed and possibly earn a podium (a prize for being in the top 3 fastest).

The 10k

The 10 km (6.2 miles) race is another popular running event with newbies and longtime runners. It has been hailed as the ideal race distance because you don't have to spend too long a training period preparing yourself and because it tests your running skills. It's challenging and tiring enough for most runners, but not as demanding in terms of training hours as the longer races. A runner can only participate in 10k races for a lifetime and still find enough to challenge him.

The half marathon (21 km)

Informally called the "half mary", this race is for more advanced runners, although it has been successfully run by beginner runners who have led active lives. In general, a person would have to run consistently for at least three months before they could start training for a half marathon. Most 21k training programs run for 12 weeks (three months) or more.

The marathon (complete) (42k)

The "full mary" (officially 42.195 km) is the pinnacle of the race that many runners aspire to finish. Ideally, a person should have been running regularly for at least 6 months (a year or more is better), before starting training for a full marathon. Most 42k training programs run for at least 16 weeks. A runner is advised to complete a few 21k races before attempting the full mary.

The word "marathon" comes from the Greek city of the same name.

Legend has it that in 490 BC, the warrior Feidippides ran from Marathon to Athens to deliver a message, and then immediately collapsed and died after doing so. He allegedly traveled a distance of 42 km without stopping.

Ultra-marathons

As grueling as they are, marathons aren't enough for the bravest and toughest runners. And so do the ultra distances, which are something longer than 42.195 km. The most popular ultra-marathons cover distances of 50 km, 50 miles (about 80 km), 100 km or 100 miles (about 161 km). Other ultra-races don't cover a precise distance, but are rather time-specific. These include 24-hour and multi-day races, where the winner is the runner who covers the longest distance within the allotted time.

All of these different races usually take place on roads, but others are on trails, which are more difficult. Many longtime road runners, once they've had a taste of trail running, find it more enjoyable due to the greater challenge and more scenic environment. They can enjoy nature to the fullest while engaging in their favorite sport.

Some races also include obstacles, both man-made and natural. A natural obstacle can be the very hot temperature in a desert run or the rough terrain on a high mountain. Man-made obstacles can include muddy areas
(present in the famous tracks in the mud), walls on which runners must climb and barbed wires under which they must crawl. These unconventional races are usually more challenging than just street races, but they can be a lot more fun too.

Is there a particular race distance you would like to train for? If you are new to running, the sensible thing would be to run shorter distances, which are 3ks and 5ks. If you are a beginner, but reasonably fit and perhaps have been athletic and active for the past few years, you can immediately do a 10k or even a half maria. Make sure, however, that you train properly by following a good training plan. In chapter 4 of this book there are some training programs for 5k, 10k, 21k and 42k distances. You can choose one or search for one online on reputable websites like Runner's World.

Another option is to join a running club if there is one in your neighborhood. Here you will meet and run with like-minded people. Many running clubs also offer free training from member coaches or more advanced and experienced member runners.

It is also a great idea to enlist the help of a professional running coach. Not only can it devise a personalized training program for you for the particular race distance you have in mind, it can also help you improve your practicing running form. It can teach you many things such as how to stretch and warm up properly, how to run faster and more efficiently, and how to deal with an injury while running. Serious runners benefit enormously from having a personal trainer. It can be a little expensive, but the benefit is worth the expense. Also, coaching doesn't have to go on for very long. Once you learn the basics, you can go back to running on your own, this time with more knowledge and confidence.

Chapter 8 - Getting started: what you need to know before traveling

Do you want to train for a particular competition? Or do you just want to start running as an exercise routine? Either way, there is a short list of things you need to know or do before you start running regularly.

Get medical approval

First on the list is, get clearance from your doctor to run if you have a health problem. This is especially important if:

are over 65 years old are overweight have lived sedentary for the past two years (do not exercise regularly) you have high blood pressure or heart problems, or if you are at risk for heart disease you are a smoker you have diabetes you have had dizziness or fainting during exercise are pregnant (healthy pregnant women can run, but to be safe, they should get their doctor's approval first).

If you are reasonably fit, or if you are doing some form of aerobic exercise regularly (cycling, rowing, using the elliptical or similar gym machine, swimming), then you can do without a visit to your doctor. You can also go if you walk regularly as a form of exercise, for about 30-45 minutes three to four times a week.

Proceed slowly and easily

If you have been inactive for a long time, gradually get back into shape by walking regularly, perhaps every other day. Do this for about two weeks, then start including short runs in your walks. For example, you can walk for five minutes, jog for a minute or two, and then repeat the cycle several times. You can use a more conservative walk-to-jog ratio if you like, such as 7-2, or a seven-minute walk followed by a two-minute run. It is important not to overload. Remember to jog only for as long as you like. If you can't speak normally (say short phrases in conversation) while jogging, you're probably overdoing it. The key is to gradually ease the ride.

Slowly but gradually increase the jogging portion of your walks until the jogging time becomes double the walking time. This means that in a 30-minute workout, you can jog for a total of 20 minutes and walk for a total of 10 minutes. Keep increasing your jogging time further until you eliminate all walking breaks and can jog for 30 minutes straight. When you can do it, you are ready to take on a 5k training program.

Get the right shoes (and other running gear)

One great thing about running is that you don't need fancy sports equipment. What you need is a good pair of running shoes. Do not use tennis shoes or trainers; it is a must that you should have proper running shoes. If you ignore this essential advice, you will likely have running injuries and you certainly don't want it.

The right shoes for you depend on your feet. You have normal (neutral) feet, flat feet, or arched feet. If you don't know your foot type, try this simple test at home: Wet the sole of one foot completely, then place yourself on a dry piece of paper. Remove your foot and study the imprint left on the paper. Compare it to the diagram below.

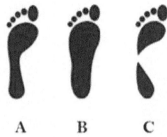

A   B   C

If your footprint resembles foot A, you have neutral feet and need neutral running shoes (or stability shoes with moderate control characteristics).

If it looks like foot B, you are flat footed and over pronate when running, so you need high stability or motion control running shoes.

If it looks like foot C, you have high arches and insufficient pronation, so you should get cushioned or flexible neutral running shoes.

When you go shopping for running shoes, tell the clerk what kind of feet you have or running shoes you need and he will be able to help you from there.

If this all sounds too complicated to you, you can simply visit a specialist running store and they will determine the type of shoe for your exact type of foot. Nowadays, running shops have computerized machines that do foot and gait analyzes for their customers and these determine which running shoes are best suited for a particular person.

Remember not to compromise on getting the right running shoes for your foot type. Running shoes aren't cheap, but they are really essential.

Later, as you become a more skilled runner, you can purchase additional shoes to complement your first pair. After a mileage of between 300 and 500 miles (approximately 500-800 km), the running shoes will still need to be replaced. There are other types of shoes you can consider, like trail or off-road shoes if you plan to run on trails and minimalist shoes if you want your shoes to be light, barely. More advanced runners generally have several pairs of running shoes; some of them are also known to use a pair exclusively for racing and other pairs for training races.

While shopping for shoes, you may also want to get hold of suitable running clothes. Lightweight, breathable tops and shorts are recommended. Consider thicker running clothes with more coverage for running in cold weather. You may also need visors or caps when running in the sun, along with good sunscreen. For the night run, choose brightly colored clothing or wear reflective materials. For long runs, also consider wearing a hydration belt. This often has a water container and a small pocket for cash and other necessities and can be worn around the waist or hip.

Other running gear like GPS watches, umbrellas, and compression garments are nice to have, but aren't as essential as shoes. You can do without it especially if you are just starting to run.

Listen to your body

It's normal to experience post-exercise pain, but watch out for other signs that may indicate overtraining or, worse, injury while running. If you are getting tired of running so much that your work or family life suffers, then you need to slow down. It could be that you are guilty of "terrible toos": going too fast and too far. It could also be that the running program you are following is too advanced for your fitness level. Or you may need a few days off from running to recover.

Pay particular attention to sharp pains or persistent discomforts that last for more than two days. Also pay attention to pains that are present only on one side of the body. Remember that normal muscle pain is often felt on both legs, not just one side.

Let your body be your boss. If it says you need to rest or slow down, don't argue with it. If you insist on running when you shouldn't, you could develop a serious injury while running that could put you on the sidelines for months. It is much, much better to take several days off than to be forced to stop running for many weeks due to an injury. Use the correct form

At first, try to run with the correct form. This will make you a more efficient runner and help you avoid injuries while running. Here are some basic guidelines:

> Keep your steps short. Don't overdo it, as this strains your legs and tires you more quickly. Even when you want to run fast, use short, quick steps rather than sweeping steps.

> When your foot lands on the ground, it shouldn't be in front of your body, but generally below your center of gravity (roughly below your hip area). This guideline also ensures that you don't overdo it.

Try developing a hit on the forefoot or midfoot. This means that the first part of the foot that should touch the ground should be the front or middle,not the heel. Running with the heel has been reported many times as the cause of some injuries while running.

Run high and lean forward slightly. Keep your head up, looking straight ahead rather than on the sidewalk a few feet away or standing. Ideally, your head, torso, hips and legs should be approximately in a straight line, leaning slightly forward from vertical.

Relax your shoulders and hands. Don't collapse forward.

Keep your elbows flexed at an angle of more or less than 90 degrees. Swing your arms naturally; when swinging forward, they should be at the sides of the body, not crossing the midline of the chest.

It is best if you can adopt the correct running form as soon as possible, before you get used to a running posture that puts unnecessary stress on your body or is not ideal in some way. Read and reread the guidelines above many times. You're not expected to be able to follow them all at once, but try to keep them in mind when running. Once in a while, while running, do a mind check of your running form and correct any mistakes you see.

Run safe

Take safety precautions when running along an unfamiliar path, at night or in the rain. Beware of dogs and vehicular traffic. If you want to listen to music on your iPod as you run, turn the volume down so you can still hear what's going on around you. You certainly don't want to miss hearing a car honking angrily behind you. Also consider wearing an identification sash that identifies you and your emergency contacts. If you can't run outdoors due to bad weather, consider running on a treadmill instead. Treadmills are also great for recovery runs because they have cushioning, thus reducing the impact on the legs.

Most importantly, relax in the first few weeks of running. Many newbies make the mistake of running too fast and too far. It is worth repeating here: avoid these "terrible toos" as much as possible. Even if you feel strong enough, don't train too much. Otherwise, you run the risk of being injured. Prevention is better than cure.

Eat sensibly

Every runner needs energy from food. This means calories. But you presumably don't want to gain weight. Maybe you might even want to lose weight, which is why you wanted to start running.

To make sure you are getting the calories you need, but not gaining weight, eat healthy complex carbohydrates like whole grains, fruits and vegetables. Eliminate unhealthy carbohydrates (cakes, white bread, pastries, chocolates, ice cream). You should also get enough unsaturated fat (good sources are avocados, olive oil, seeds, and nuts) and muscle-repairing protein (consider fish, eggs, beans, and lean poultry).

Stay hydrated throughout the day, especially while running. Water is good for you, but you also need electrolytes to fuel your runs, so take sports and energy drinks on your runs. Later we will discuss what you need to eat and drink on race day and during training.

Be patient

If you are trying to lose weight, you may be discouraged if you don't see results after a few weeks of running. Weight loss can only happen when you exercise and eat more sensibly. Many runners don't actually lose weight when they continue to eat as they did before, even with the additional exercise. Exercise alone is not enough. Diet also needs to be changed.

This does not mean, however, that everything they do is for nothing. Many improvements are taking place within the body, although these may not be evident on the scale or in the mirror. Your muscles, tendons, and ligaments are getting stronger; your bones are growing and becoming harder and denser; your blood is able to carry more oxygen and nutrients; the cells in your body are becoming more energized as they develop more mitochondria; and your body's ability to use fat as fuel is significantly increased. You certainly get healthier and stronger when you run.

But if it's the weight loss you want to see, be patient. Reduce your total calorie intake, but without compromising your running energy needs. In due course, you will lose a few pounds, but you will have to work on it with both diet and exercise.

Chapter 9 - How to train

It's ideal if you can run regularly and make it your exercise habit. This means you should run three or more times a week, with each run lasting at least 30 minutes. That way, you'll reap the benefits of good health and eventual weight loss (if you also look at what you eat). It's okay if you take a few days off because you feel tired or busy, as long as you get back to running regularly once you are able to do it again.

After a while, you will definitely feel the need to sign up for a race. For starters, a 5k is recommended, but if you are fit enough and have been running long enough, you can do a 10k or even a 21k as your first race. Regardless of the distance you choose, definitely register for a race. Races are highlights in the life of every runner. They should be tried at least once.

In this chapter you will find example training programs for 5k, 10k, 21k and 42k distances. These are all meant for beginners, i.e. those who are attempting the given distance for the first time.

Once you've done two or more 5ks and want to run the same distance again, you should choose a training program for intermediate or advanced runners. The same goes for the other race distances.

Also specified in the training programs below are the preconditions or mileage for each race distance. Remember that you shouldn't run right after you start running regularly. You should accumulate enough miles before you sign up for a race and start training.

Training plans

A training program is what a runner follows to train for a certain race distance. The training programs are designed for different levels of running, from beginner / beginner to advanced. Many programs are available online; feel free to browse them until you find the one that best suits your schedule and skills. Many of these programs are free, while others require payment.

You can also choose one of the training programs listed below. These are designed for beginners. We have intentionally included several styles of training plans, so you can get an idea of the variety available. You will notice that some plans are simpler and easier to follow than others. Many runners prefer these, but others prefer to follow a more precise and detailed program. As the saying goes, they are different traits for different people. Choose the training plan you like and stick to it for a successful 5k, 10k, 21k or 42k first race.

5k training program for beginners

This is a two month program that will allow you to complete a 5km race.

Before starting week 1 of the program, you should be able to perform at least

2 km continuously, without taking a walking break. This roughly translates to 15-20 minutes of straight running. If you can run longer, that's a lot better.

This schedule assumes your day off is Sunday. So do your longest runs on this day. Another critical day is Wednesday, when you also run long runs. If this schedule is not convenient for you, you can change the days to assign a day other than Sunday or Wednesday as the long run day. But stick to the original sequence of days and workouts as shown in the program.

Warm-up and cool-down exercises are not included in the program. You should do this in addition to the indicated rides. In fact, in every run, even when you're not training for a race, you should warm up first and cool down later. A simple jog and a few stretching movements are great exercises for these.

Cross-training (CT) days are included in the program. On this day, you can do other aerobic exercises like biking, swimming, Zumba, dancing, or just walking. Only 30-45 minutes of CT is enough. Another option is to do strength training in the gym. This is very useful for runners.

Thursdays are designated as days off or CT. If you feel tired, give up crosstraining and rest. Tuesdays and Saturdays are also days of rest.

W	Mon	Tue	Wed	Thu	Fri	Sat	Sun
1	Easy run: 20-30 minutes, or cross-train (CT)		Run: 2 km		Run: 2 km		Run: 2.5 km
2	Easy run: 20-30 minutes, or CT		Run: 2.5 km		Run: 2.5 km		Run: 3 km
3	Easy run: 20-30 minutes, or CT		Run: 3 km		Run: 2.5 km		Run: 3.5 km
4	Easy run: 25-35 minutes, or CT	Rest	Run: 3.5 km	CT or Rest	Run: 2.5 km	Rest	Run: 4 km
5	Easy run: 25-35 minutes, or CT		Run: 4 km		Run: 3 km		Run: 4.5 km
6	Easy run: 35-40 minutes, or CT		Run: 4.5 km		Run: 3 km		Run: 4.5 km
7	Easy run: 35-40 minutes, or CT		Run: 5 km		Run: 3 km		Run: 5 km
8	Rest		Run: 3 km		Run: 3 km		Race Day

Note that the program includes only basic and repair runs. You don't have to do timed runs and intervals or uphill repeats just yet. You will do this when you train for longer distances.

It is important to take things calmly and rest often. This is just your first race, so enjoy the experience and don't get too stressed out.

Don't worry about making a good race time (the time by which you finish the 5k). For your first race, the important thing is to reach the finish line strong, without injuries and smiling. It doesn't matter if you do it within 30 minutes, 45 minutes, or an hour or more. It is in the next 5k that you should strive to improve your finish time.

10k training program for beginners

This is a three month program that will allow you to finish a 10k race. It consists of basic runs, reset runs and CTs. It also includes speed and fartlek workouts, which are not found in the 5k program shown above.

To find out if you're ready for this program, set aside at least two weeks of pre-workout. In these two weeks, run 5km once and 7km four times a week. This means a total of five runs and two rest days in one week. If you can do it without hurting yourself or experiencing great discomfort, you are ready for this 10km training program. If you can't, give yourself more time to become a stronger runner. Keep running and accumulating miles and return to the pre-workout test after some time.

For this 10k training program, you will need to know your 5k or 10k pace.
This is simply the approximate speed at which you can run a 5 or 10km race. You can measure this using the result of the 5k race (divide the finish time by 5km). If you don't have it, you can run the distance (5k) and time yourself or use a GPS watch to determine your average pace on that run.
Alternatively, you can use smartphone apps that can measure your pace and distance during any outdoor run. You can try the RunKeeper and Nike + apps, which are free to download and work on Android and Apple phones. They use GPS technology to track distance, pace, time and other running metrics.

In this program, you will be doing your longest runs on Sundays. Do it calmly or calmly. Note that you will actually have some Sunday runs that exceed 10km.

On Tuesdays you will do fartleks, intervals and uphill reps. For fartleks, add a warm-up run and a 1.5km cool-down run before and after. "4-5 hills" means you should do 4 to 5 reps uphill. The hills are ideally short (about 200 meters) but with an upward slope. The "long hills" are about 500 yards long. For interval runs, "5 x 440" means you should do 5 reps of 440 yards each. The latter should be done on a track, where one lap is 440 yards and two laps of 880 yards. You can rest a minute or two between each interval.

Tuesday runs with a * should be done at your 5K or 10K pace.

You will have two days off: Monday and Friday.

W	Mon	Tue	Wed	Thu	Fri	Sat	Sun
1		6.5 km	5 km	6.5 km		6.5 km	6.5 km
2		Fartlek (6.5 km)	6.5 km	5 km		5 km	8 km
3		Fartlek (6.5 km)	6.5 km	5 km		5 km	9.5 km
4		4-5 hills *	5 km	6.5 km		6.5 km	11 km
5	Rest	5 x 440s *	6.5 km	8 km	Rest	6.5 km	9.5 km
6		3-4 Long Hills *	6.5 km	8 km		5 km	11 km
7		8 km	5 km	8 km		5 km	13 km
8		4-5 Long Hills *	5 km	6.5 km		5 km	11 km
9		6.5 km	5 km	6 x 880s *		6.5 km	9.5 km
10		5 x 440s *	5 km	8 km		6.5 km	8 km
11		5 x 880s *	5 km	6.5 km		5 km	8 km
12		Fartlek (6.5 km)	5 km	5 km		3 km	RACE DAY

21k training program for beginners

This is a relatively easy 14-week training program for a 21km race. Includes cross training (CT) days for non-running exercises such as dance, yoga, swimming, badminton, cycling and others. It also includes strength training (ST) days, during which you should do pushups, crunches, planks, lunges, squats, and core-strengthening exercises. About 20 minutes of these are recommended. Strength training, especially on the core and arm areas, is extremely beneficial for runners.

All runs in this program are easy basic runs, unless otherwise indicated. RW are runs that can include walking portions so that the runner can catch his breath. They are meant to be even easier than the easy basic runs. BW are fast walks, intended as a recovery exercise. Saturday is the day of long runs and Sunday is reserved for fast recovery walks.

This program is perfect for women and beginner runners. It's not as demanding as other floors, but it's enough to prepare anyone to reach the finish line in a 21km race.

W	Mon	Tue	Wed	Thu	Fri	Sat	Sun
1		RW 3 km	CT 30 mins	RW 3 km		RW 5 km	BW 3 km
2		RW 5 km + ST	CT 30 mins	RW 3 km		RW 5 km	BW 3 km
3		RW 5 km + ST	CT 30 mins	RW 3 km		RW 5 km	BW 3 km
4		Run 3 km + ST	CT 30 mins	Run 5 km		Run 6.5 km	BW 5 km
5	Rest	Run 5 km + ST	CT 40 mins	Run 5 km	Rest or CT	Run 8 km	RW 5 km
6		Run 5 km + ST	CT 40 mins	Run 5 km		Run 9.5 km	RW 5 km
7		Run 6.5 km + ST	CT 40 mins	Run 6.5 km		Run 11 km	RW 5 km
8		Run 6.5 km + ST	CT 40 mins	Tempo Run 6.5 km		Run 13 km	RW 5 km
9		Run 6.5 km + ST	CT 45 mins	Tempo Run 6.5 km		Run 14.5 km	RW 6.5 km
10		Run 6.5 km + ST	CT 45 mins	Tempo Run 6.5 km		Run 16 km	RW 5 km
11		Run 6.5 km + ST	CT 40 mins	Tempo Run 6.5 km		Run 16 km	RW 5 km
12		Run 6.5 km + ST	CT 40 mins	Tempo Run 6.5 km		Run 17.5 km	RW 5 km
13		Run 6.5 km + ST	CT 40 mins	Run 6.5 km		Run 9.5 km	RW 5 km
14		Run 6.5 km	Rest	Run 5 km		Run 3 km	Race Day

42k training program for beginners

Below is an easy-to-follow sofa-to-marathon training program. It is one of the very popular Hal Higdon training programs that beginners prefer for their ease and simplicity.

It covers 18 weeks and mainly consists of easy runs. It also features crosstraining days (Sunday). Timed runs or uphill repetitions are not included, but a 21km race is. The program recommends that the runner run a half marathon on Sunday of week 8. If that can't be done, a simple 21k LSD will suffice that day.

Mondays and Fridays are rest days, while long runs are scheduled on Saturdays.

W	Mon	Tue	Wed	Thu	Fri	Sat	Sun
1		5 km	5 km	5 km		9.5 km	CT
2		5 km	5 km	5 km		11 km	CT
3		5 km	6.5 km	5 km		8 km	CT
4		5 km	6.5 km	5 km		14.5 km	CT
5		5 km	8 km	5 km		16 km	CT
6		5 km	8 km	5 km		11 km	CT
7	Rest	5 km	9.5 km	5 km	Rest	19 km	CT
8		5 km	9.5 km	5 km		Rest	Half Marathon Race
9		5 km	11 km	6.5 km		16 km	CT
10		5 km	11 km	6.5 km		24 km	CT
11		6.5 km	13 km	6.5 km		25.5 km	CT
12		6.5 km	13 km	8 km		19 km	CT
13		6.5 km	14.5 km	8 km		19 km	CT
14		8 km	14.5 km	8 km		22.5 km	CT
15		8 km	16 km	8 km		32 km	CT
16		8 km	13 km	6.5 km		19 km	CT
17		6.5 km	9.5 km	5 km		13 km	CT
18		5 km	6.5 km	3 km		Rest	Race Day

Chapter 10 - Smart Training: Tips for Getting the Most Out of Training

To train properly, it is not enough to follow a certain training program. You should also eat right, get enough sleep, and hydrate adequately while running. We will explain these points and talk about other essential running tips in this chapter.

The importance of pre-competition training

Your training will determine what happens on race day. Your success in completing a given race distance depends on the many weeks and months you train before the race. Training is therefore essential. If you have trained poorly, you will have less chance of running successfully. But if you have trained well, you will have a great chance of finishing well, even if you will feel bad and weak on the day of the competition. This is what coaches mean when they say races are won or lost before race day.

The key point to remember is, don't run a race that you haven't trained properly for. If you do, you are bracing yourself for a disappointing experience and even a potentially serious injury.

Get enough mileage

"Take what you put on," goes the common adage. This is certainly true in running. A basic rule of thumb for any runner is that they should accumulate a sufficient base of miles before they start running or before attempting longer and faster distances.

Survey studies have shown that the runners who run the fastest marathons are the ones who have the most total miles per week. Runners who run approximately 60 to 70km per week have the fastest average finish line of the marathon. Meanwhile, runners who have the lowest weekly mileage (10km or less) have the slowest finish times.

But how much mileage is really enough? Here are some rules to keep in mind:

The mileage required depends on the race distance. The longer the ride, the greater the mileage.

More mileage is required if the runner wishes to improve his previous record. To get a faster finish time or personal best (PR), he should run more. It should also have more "quality runs" that include times, intervals and uphill repetitions, not just basic runs done at an easy pace. It should be remembered, however, that more demanding runs require more rest and recovery, so balance needs to be found to avoid over-training and the development of injuries.

Here are some recommended weekly mileage totals:

Target race distance	Weekly mileage
5k	32-40 km
10k	40-48 km
21k	48-64 km
42k	48-80 km

Sleep and nutritional requirements

Getting enough sleep each night is of paramount importance for runners. It becomes especially essential around race day. Therefore, many runners have developed the habit of waking up early (for a morning run) and going to bed early (to get enough sleep). Not getting enough sleep can seriously reduce any runner's performance on race day.

The carbohydrate and protein requirement of runners is greater than that of people who are not physically active. Make sure you're getting enough carbohydrates from healthy sources, such as fruits, vegetables, and whole grains. These should make up about 65% of the total food intake. Protein, meanwhile, should make up about 15% of the daily intake. Good sources of protein are lean meat, fish, beans and poultry. You need enough protein for muscle and tissue recovery and repair. Other nutritional needs of runners are fats (about 20%) and vitamins and minerals, especially vitamins C and E, and calcium, iron and sodium.

During runs, the person should drink enough water and energy drinks to have enough fuel. A rough guide is that he should drink at least 4 ounces every 2-3 miles. If the run exceeds an hour or 90 minutes, she should also be eating solid food. Bananas, energy bars, and sports gels and jellies are some easily digestible foods that are great during runs. The rule of thumb is that you should eat about 100 calories after an hour of running, and then another 100 calories for every 45 minutes thereafter. If you run hard and fast, you may need more.

Remember to refuel before and after a run as well. Ideally, you should eat some carbohydrates about 45 minutes before a run; it doesn't have to be a meal, just enough food to get your metabolism working and to give you enough energy to start running, especially if you're going for a morning run. Then, within 30 minutes of finishing a run, you should take recovery food to replenish the glycogen supply to your muscles.

During a run, some runners prefer to hydrate and eat depending on how they feel. That is, they drink when they are thirsty and eat when they feel hungry or weak. It is best to drink before you feel thirsty and have solid food before your legs and knees drop from fatigue. Remember that your muscles can't move if they don't have enough fuel. They will crack if you don't provide this necessary fuel, and that's something you really want to avoid.

Experiment during your training sessions to find out which foods and drinks suit you best and how often to take them. The important thing is never to run on an empty stomach. The runners actually died from dehydration and a lack of electrolytes in their body.

Once you find out which fuel works best for you, stick to it on race day. Do not experiment with new foods or drinks on race day, as this may upset your stomach or cause some discomfort which will reduce your race performance.

CHAPTER 11

All about nutrition

Whether your goal is to run short distances, long distances or all distances, your nutritional intake is critical to both your performance and how well you feel before, during and after a run. The information contained in this chapter is a guide on what and how to eat to feel your best and give your best in races and races. It will also describe some of the popular diets for runners along with special considerations for women.

The nutritional mindset

Do you have the nutrition mindset? Do you think about what, when and how you eat? Do you have a goal of optimizing your diet to fuel your muscles to function efficiently every day? The nutritional mindset starts with understanding how the body wants to be fed while at rest and with activity. It's about understanding the value of the different foods you have available and choosing the right balance and the right quantities at the right times every day.

According to Merriam Webster's definition, nutrition is the act or process of nurturing or being nurtured; in particular, the sum of the processes by which an animal or a plant absorbs and uses food substances. You eat to fuel every organ in your body for energy and function.

The nutritional mindset is eating for health and performance each and every day, not just before a race. When you eat a healthy diet every day, you feed your muscles and organs with protective nutrients that are the foundation of optimal performance, good health and feeling good!

The balanced diet

What is a calorie?

Technically, a food calorie is a unit of energy, the amount of energy needed to raise the temperature of a kilogram of water by 1 degree Celsius. The number of calories in a serving of food tells us how much energy a food potentially provides the body. If this energy is not being used by the body, it usually is stored in the body as fat for later use. Calories are used to fuel the body, including the heart, lungs, brain, and skeletal muscles. The number of calories we need varies based on our age, gender, size, health and activity level.

A balanced diet means more than a plate of food that meets different nutritional needs. It means eating this plate of food or a mini-plate of this food regularly spaced throughout the day, starting with the first thing in the morning (breakfast). Since the goal is to eat moderate amounts every time you eat, you are likely consuming a plate or mini-plate of food three to six times a day.

Let's analyze this dish further to better understand the nutrients needed for running. There are six nutrients needed to sustain life: water, carbohydrates, proteins, fats, vitamins and minerals.

water

Water is the most important nutrient for the body. Your body is 60-70% water and without water you would die. Water is responsible for transporting other nutrients to the muscles and eliminating waste through the kidneys and other organs for disposal. Water lubricates the joints and helps cushion the organs of the body. Water helps regulate body temperature. Water is also essential for maintaining healthy skin.

Carbohydrates

The main function of carbohydrates is to provide energy to the body, especially energy for the functioning of the brain and nervous system. Carbohydrates also provide energy to the muscles needed during activity. Foods containing carbohydrates are classified as complex and simple carbohydrates. Complex carbohydrates are generally referred to as starches. They form when sugars join together to form a complex chain of sugar molecules. Potatoes, rice, pasta, bread, legumes and other starchy vegetables are referred to as complex carbohydrates. Simple carbohydrates are sugars like table sugar, corn syrup, honey, and even milk sugar, as well as fruits, juices, and some vegetables.

Diet drink is the non-digestible portion of fruits, vegetables and grains. Fiber has many benefits such as promoting normal bowel movements, regulating blood sugar, lowering cholesterol, and reducing the risk of some cancers. Fiber holds water as it moves through the digestive system. Make sure you drink enough fluids when on a rich diet.

Carbohydrates can also be classified based on the rate of absorption. Fast-absorbing carbohydrates quickly raise blood sugar levels. These carbohydrates are great carbohydrates for recovery after a run. Examples of fast-absorbing carbohydrates include baked potatoes,   honey,   white   bread,   is   re   ned   cereal.   Slow   carbohydrates   are digested more slowly and cause a more gradual rise in blood sugar. These slow-absorbing carbohydrates are more sustainable and are best consumed before exercise for sustained energy. Examples of slow-absorbing carbohydrates include apples, apricots, oatmeal, and dried beans.

Protein

Proteins are the building blocks of muscles and are present in every cell in the body, including organs, hair and skin. Proteins are made up of amino acids. There are eight essential amino acids needed to form the protein found in muscles, organs, hormones and enzymes. These eight amino acids must come from your diet as your body cannot make them. Food sources of protein that contain all essential amino acids include meat, fish, poultry, eggs, dairy, and soy. Grains and other plant foods do not contain all of the essential amino acids and must be combined with other foods containing the missing amino acids to form a complete protein.

Fat

Fat is a nutrient that is part of every cell membrane. Fat contains essential fatty acids necessary for the production of hormones. Fat in the diet allows fat-soluble vitamins (vitamins A, D, E and K) to be absorbed into the body. Fat is often misunderstood because fat has been associated with heart disease. Through decades of research we have now understood that monounsaturated and polyunsaturated fats are protective and important in a healthy diet, while saturated fats are bad for our health. Examples of monounsaturated fats are olive oil, canola oil, and walnuts. Polyunsaturated fats are made up of corn oil, soybean oil and fatty fish. Examples of saturated fats are butter, cream, cheese, and meat fat.

Hydrogenated fats are processed fats that act similarly to saturated fats. Hydrogenation is the process of adding hydrogen to polyunsaturated fats to give food a longer shelf life and to add flavor. Baked goods such as cookies and crackers, margarines and some peanut butters contain hydrogenated or partially hydrogenated fats.

Vitamins and minerals

Both vitamins and minerals are necessary for life. The body cannot produce vitamins and minerals. Vitamins are sometimes referred to as the "candles" of our diet: vitamins are effective in allowing our body to release energy but do not contain any energy value in and of themselves. Minerals support life processes such as blood oxygenation, heart rhythm and bone structure. The best way to consume vitamins and minerals is through a healthy and balanced diet.

Eat well to run and compete

The composition of the diet for a runner consists of eating mainly carbohydrates, a moderate amount of protein and limited fat. Eating well for running and racing requires adequate hydration and sufficient fuel consumption for the muscles.

Moisturize properly

The only main reason for poor running performance is soon fatigue is related to poor hydration. Dehydration affects running performance when you lose only 2% of your body weight in water. Choosing mostly water along with fruit, fruit juices, and dairy products throughout the day helps keep you well hydrated. As soon as you are dehydrated, your heart needs to work harder, your body temperature rises and you start to feel sick. In non-athletic conditions, the rule of thumb is to drink eight 8-ounce glasses of uid per day, which protects most people from dehydration. With physical activity, the amount you need to drink increases. Unfortunately, during exercise, the body's thirst mechanism may not be a good guide. Instead of relying totally on thirst,

Calculation of the sweating rate

Your sweating rate will vary based on weather conditions. During the calculation your sweat rate, run your normal running pace for 1 hour in a variety of temperature and humidity conditions. Complete the following steps.

> **First step:** Take your naked weight before and after a run and see the difference in ounces.
>
> **Step two:** Add to this the amount of uid you drank during the run.
>
> **Step three:** Take this amount and divide by 4 to determine how much you should drink every 15 minutes.

EXAMPLE

Weight before: 200 lbs. Weight after: 199 lbs.
Drink: 8 ounces of water
Sweat loss: 24 ounces / hour

Divide your hourly uid loss by 4 = 6 ounces every 15 minutes.

Coffee drinks were once thought to dehydrate rather than hydrate the body. Recent studies have shown that the ca eine in popular beverages does not prevent the body from absorbing fluids and ca eined beverages can be regarded as fluid intake. Coffee drinks, however, should not be used as the sole moisturizer.

If your weight after running is greater than your weight before running, you may be drinking too much while running. Your post-run weight should be the same or within 1 to 2 pounds less than your pre-run weight.

For runs lasting more than 1 hour, we recommend using a sports drink containing carbohydrates, liquids and sodium. Carbohydrates help prevent muscle glycogen depletion, fluids keep you hydrated, and sodium keeps your electrolytes in balance. (Electrolytes are chemicals in the body that carry electrical charges necessary for cellular function and for utilizing caloric energy.)

Adequate fuel

When you run, your body relies on stored carbohydrates and fats to give you energy. Even the leanest runner has enough fat reserves to run, yet when you run out of carbs, you "hit the wall." Carbohydrates are stored in the muscles and liver in the form of glycogen, which breaks down into sugar for use as energy. Adequate levels of glycogen are critical for a successful run. Glycogen capacity improves through a combination of an adequate carbohydrate diet and through training. Both diet and training optimize the amount of glycogen your muscles can store.

Looking at ChooseMyPlate.gov, you'll see that three-quarters of the plate is made up of carbohydrate foods (fruits, vegetables, and grains), which equates to about 50 percent of the calorie intake from carbohydrates. Look at your "plate of food" to see if you have enough carbohydrates. Fruits, starchy vegetables such as beans, peas, potatoes and corn, along with breads and cereals, have a higher carbohydrate content per serving than non-starchy "green" vegetables. When evaluating your meal, make sure it is not made entirely of green salad ingredients or you will not be consuming enough carbohydrates.

Before, during and after the race

How you feed your body before, during and after your run makes a difference in how you feel and how you perform.

Before your run

Follow these guidelines as you prepare for your workout.

Moisturizer before the run

As mentioned above, if you start your run fully hydrated you will be more successful. A rule of thumb is to consume 14-20 ounces of water or sports drink 2-3 hours before running. Drink 8 ounces before starting your run. The best way to know if you're drinking enough is to notice the color of your urine. If darker than pale yellow, you need more uid; if your urine is completely clean, you may be drinking too much before running.

Refueling before the race

The amount of food you eat before a run varies based on the time of the run. A moderate sized meal is best consumed 3-4 hours before a run. If there are only 2 hours between the meal and the ride, the portion should be less. If you're short on time before your run, you'll only have room for a snack. The point is that the food is fully digested before you run so that the fuel you just consumed provides energy for your working muscles. Your pre-run meal should consist of the components of a balanced meal while minimizing fat and beer to minimize digestive discomfort. Liquid meals can be better tolerated when the food is consumed closer to running. The small amount of protein in the pre-run meal helps build and repair muscle tissue and can help with post-exercise pain. Examples of pre-run food include a peanut butter and jelly sandwich,

A small percentage of runners may experience rebound hypoglycemia when they consume a sugary snack 30-60 minutes before running. Symptoms can include weakness, dizziness, tremor, and heart palpitations while running. Solutions include using a slow-absorbing carbohydrate source as a snack or, better yet, being prepared with regularly spaced meals and snacks 1-2 hours before your run.

Frequent questions

I just woke up from bed and walked out the door for my run. How can I eat?

If you've just woken up you can be sure your glycogen stores are below optimal. If you don't have much time before your run, consume at least 8 ounces of a carbohydrate-based liquid drink before taking your first steps.

Eating before running gives me GI distress.

If you can't eat anything before your morning run, make sure your early evening meal was enough. It may also be helpful to have a mini meal before bed. Make sure you consume water before starting your run. Additionally, some people cannot eat before a run but can eat gastrointestinal problems while running. Keep a source of carbohydrates with you while running.

I run right after work and I'm already starving.

When you run after work, make sure you have a mid-afternoon snack that is sufficient in carbohydrates but with some protein to support you during the afternoon. When you get too hungry, you're more likely to reach for a high-fat food source right before your run, causing stomach pain during or after your run.

During the ride

You must use the following instructions when exercising.

Moisturizer while running

For any run that lasts longer than 20 minutes, hydration while running is important. In cold conditions, you may not need to hydrate during a 30–45 minute run. But if the heat and / or humidity is high, don't trust your thirst. The American College of Sports Medicine recommends that athletes consume fluids at a rate close to their sweating rate, which for the most part is 3-7 ounces every 15 minutes.

Refueling during the race

Fuel your body with 30–60 grams of fast-absorbing carbohydrates for every hour of running. Ideally, this is broken down into 10-20 grams of carbohydrates every 20 minutes. Your fuel can be in the form of a carbohydrate drink, gel, jelly, fruit or carbohydrate snack, depending on your preferences and tolerance. Experiment with sports drinks and bars during your training sessions to find out what works best for you. Refueling while running may consist of sports drinks, fruit slices, gels, chewing gum, or low-fat sports bites or granola bars.

The optimal concentration of carbohydrates in a sports drink should be 4-8%, or 10-18 grams per 8 ounces. The best carbohydrate sources include a combination of glucose, maltodextrin, sucrose, and dextrose. Sports drinks that only contain electrolytes are not enough for runs that last longer than 45

minutes unless another carbohydrate source is ingested, such as gels, bars, chews, or fruit.

Consider this

I drink a lot of water during my 2 hour runs but I don't eat. Is there a problem with that?

Running long distances and consuming only water can lead to a condition called hyponatremia. Hyponatremia is a condition in which there is too little sodium in the blood. Sodium is lost in sweat and regular water consumed in excess during a run dilutes the sodium balance. Even if you are well acclimatized, it is always a good idea to use resistance drinks that contain adequate sodium and necessary carbohydrates.

After the run

Follow these tips to ensure safe recovery after you're done your ride.

Moisturizer after running

Continue drinking fluids after your run. Be careful to your urge to urinate and notice its color. You should urinate within 1 hour of completing your run. Keep drinking fluids until the color of your urine turns pale yellow.

Refueling after the race

Whenever you run, glycogen stores are depleted, fluids and electrolytes are lost, and muscle fibers are damaged. As soon as you complete your run, think about recovery. Nutrition is as important right after running as it was before and during running. Quickly replenishing the body after running harnesses the body's ability to repair and restore optimal levels. Fuel your body within 30 minutes of running with a protein, carbohydrate, and liquid snack. Look for foods that provide at least 10 grams of protein. Protein helps in the repair of damaged muscle tissue and stimulates the development of new tissue. Consume 30–50 grams of carbohydrates to replenish depleted glycogen and also to improve muscle repair.

What should I look for in an energy bar?

The energy bar you choose depends on its purpose. First

and during exercise, choose energy bars that provide primarily carbohydrates and are low in ber and fat. For post-exercise and between-meal snacks, choose energy bars that contain at least a 1: 3 ratio of protein to carbohydrate with less than 30% of the calories coming from fat.

Post-execution scenario

I get nauseous after running and can't eat anything for a few hours. What can I do to get into my post-run diet?

If you feel nauseous after running, think about what you eat and drink before and during your run. Before your run, be sure to consume easily digestible foods that are low in fat and fiber. While running, experiment with other drinks and carbohydrate sources to see if others are better tolerated. At the end of the run, try drinking 4-8 ounces of a carbonated drink like ginger ale or even a cola to calm your stomach. You will consume this drink by ingesting carbohydrates and uid. If it works, you can switch to a healthier snack or meal for a continued replenishment.

What do "real" runners eat?

Who are you looking for nutritional advice? Do you look at other runners? Below are two runners who have done well in their sport.

Mary is a 40-year-old runner who has run her entire adult life. He trains for a half marathon a year and otherwise runs 5K and 10K races. Mary stands 55 tall and weighs 130 pounds. His best running times occurred when he was 30. He has often won his age group in local races.

Mary's typical daily diet consisted of:

Breakfast: Coffee, 2 cups of chopped wheat, 1 cup of milk, 1 banana, ¼ cup of walnuts

Mid-morning snack: A 200 calorie snack made from yogurt and mixed fruit

Lunch: Turkey and cheese sandwich with mayonnaise, pretzels, apple, 2 medium cookies

Afternoon snack: Almonds and pretzels

Dinner: Chicken breast, baked potatoes with butter, 1 cup of broccoli, corn on the cob, glass of wine

Snack before bedtime: 2 cookies and a glass of skim milk

The night before a race, Mary would have done best with a small lean steak, a large baked potato, green beans and water. The common prerace pasta dinner wasn't just for her.

Mary was a consistent eater and a consistent runner. Though a careful evaluation might show areas for improvement in her diet, she followed a diet she enjoyed and was considerate in what worked for her (steak over pasta). It provided her body with nutrients and energy and kept her weight steady. Good boy!

John is a 35 year old runner who ran weekly with Mary. John once won local races or finished in the top five when he was 20. John lives on sports drinks, granola bars, jellies and burgers. Here is John's typical daily intake:

> **Breakfast:** 2 cereal bars and 16 ounces of Midmorning Sports Drink: Jellybeans and 16 ounces of Sports Drink
> **Lunch:** Burgers and fries and 16 ounces of sports drinks

Afternoon snack: 16 ounces of sports drink and a cereal bar
Dinner: Chicken sandwich and fries, iced tea
Before going to bed: 16 ounces of sports drink

John had the genetic advantage. Yet as John got older, his weight increased and his times got slower. Both her weight and her nutrition likely contributed to her slower performance. Now he is working to eat smarter and asks Mary for advice.

"Real" runners eat in a variety of ways, sometimes following what research tells us is useful and healthy, sometimes not. For the best chance of optimal performance and energy, however, follow sports nutrition guidelines, not necessarily what your running mates eat.

Popular diets

Runners often seek the magic bullet to help them run faster, become leaner, and feel better. This makes diet books and supplements attractive. But do they work? Let's take a look at the evidence of some popular diets.

The Paleolithic diet

The Paleolithic diet is often abbreviated as the paleo diet. It is the diet plan that best resembles how the first cavemen ate thousands of years ago, eating plants and wildlife. Meat, fish, shellfish, eggs, nuts, vegetables, roots, fruits and berries are allowed, while cereals and dairy products are prohibited. One of the main benefits of this diet is that processed foods are eliminated and foods rich in proteins, vitamins, minerals, phytochemicals, and antioxidants are consumed.

The creators of the Paleo diet adapted it for athletes, recognizing that athletes need more carbohydrates before, during and after exercise. The Paleo diet for athletes allows for the inclusion of higher glycemic grains and carbohydrates, especially for recovery after exercise.

If you are on a Paleo diet, you need to consume enough variety to get all the nutrients needed for optimal health. Following this diet by picking and choosing only certain foods can lead to deficiencies. Since it is more difficult to consume enough calcium and vitamin D on this diet, it may be wise to take a calcium and vitamin D supplement. There is currently no conclusive evidence that this particular diet is superior to others in optimizing health and performance. .

The raw food diet

Raw food is a belief that plant foods in their most natural state are the healthiest for the body. The raw food diet consists of 75% fruits and vegetables. Food choices include seaweed, sprouts, whole grains, beans, and nuts. Food preparation involves a dehydrator that heats to a temperature no higher than 118 degrees Fahrenheit so that vitamins, minerals, and food enzymes are not destroyed.

Although many benefits can be obtained through a diet rich in fruits and vegetables, some fruits and vegetables are more available to the body when cooked. For example, the lycopene in tomatoes is most beneficial to the body when tomatoes are cooked. Foods prepared at temperatures of 118 degrees or below may not destroy all harmful food-borne bacteria and can be dangerous. People following this diet may have di culty in getting enough vitamin B12, calcium, iron and omega-3 fatty acids, thus requiring supplementation.

Special considerations for female athletes

Males and females are not built equally. The ideal body compositions of a male and female body are quite different. In contrast to a male, whose body is made up of 3–5 percent essential fat, the essential fat of a female body is 11–13 percent. Body fat serves a purpose - to cushion the organs - and in females it prepares the body for reproduction. Although variable, most women require a minimum of 17% body fat for normal menstruation. And, while many women don't mind not having menstrual periods, the monthly cycle does more for a female than preparing her for reproduction. Among many functions, the hormones associated with a menstrual period, especially estrogen, are important for the growth and development of the brain and bones. Females with low body fat and no menstrual cycle (amenorrhea) are more likely to have stress fractures, premature osteoporosis, and an inability to conceive. The combination of low body weight (low body fat) and amenorrhea is a strong predictor of osteoporosis, regardless of the amount of exercise under load or calcium consumed in the diet.

The triad of the female athlete

For some runners, most commonly women, running is not just an enjoyable activity that increases tension and reduces stress, it is a means to an end: to lose weight and above all to lose body fat. Although males and females alike seek to have a lean body, the female runner tends to have a greater obsession and drive towards thinness. Low caloric intake and high energy expenditure deriving from physical exercise, or a deficient and disordered diet; osteoporosis or weakened bones; and amenorrhea results in what is called the female athletic triad. Excessive exercise without sufficient fuel results in impaired nutritional status, premature fatigue, immune suppression, bone loss, stress fractures, and osteoporosis. The body requires a certain number of calories just for vital bodily processes to occur. About 70 percent of the calorie requirement is used to feed vital organs (heart, lungs, kidneys, liver, brain). You deprive your vital organs of the energy they need when you only eat enough calories to make up for the calories burned during exercise.

Some women and a growing number of men pushed to thinness and body image struggle with disordered eating and even eating disorders that trap them in an obsession with undernourishment and overexertion. Although it is commonly believed that disordered eating occurs predominantly among women, the National Eating Disorders Association estimates that more than 1 million men and boys in the United States also struggle with eating disorders. If you find yourself in this unhealthy trap, seek help.

Iron deficiency anemia

Another problem that occurs more often with females than males is iron deficiency anemia. When iron stores are low, fatigue increases and performance suffers. Iron is a component of hemoglobin, the red blood cell protein that moves oxygen through the blood from the lungs to the working muscles. Without adequate oxygen to move to the working muscles, you cannot perform at your best and live in a state of fatigue. The recommended amount of iron to consume each day is 8 milligrams for men and 18 milligrams for menstruating women. Postmenopausal women should consume 8 milligrams of iron per day.

Female athletes are at high risk of developing iron deficiency anemia due to iron loss through monthly menstrual bleeding, along with the breakdown of iron-containing red blood cells that occurs after a foot strike against the floor while running. Endurance athletes can also lose iron through sweat. If you feel fatigued easily, it's a good idea to ask your doctor to check your iron status, and in particular your ferritin levels. Ferritin, a protein that binds to iron, measures the iron stores in your body. Checking ferritin levels is not routine but can reveal a state of pre-anemia.

There are many self-proclaimed "nutritionists" who give advice on sports nutrition. When looking for reliable information, look for a "Registered Dietitian" or "RD" who specializes in sports nutrition.

Iron is best consumed through lean cuts of beef, pork, lamb, chicken, and turkey. Iron in animal foods is better absorbed into the body than plant sources of iron, such as dark green leafy vegetables such as spinach. Iron can also be obtained in enriched and fortified breads and cereals. Using a cast iron skillet for cooking allows food to absorb iron for greater benefit. Coffee and tea inhibit iron absorption and are best consumed one hour before or after a meal.

Chapter 12

YOUR TRAINING PROGRAM

If you still don't have a clue as to where to
start and how to incorporate these types of
training into your running routine to train
yourself to run farther and faster, then
hopefully these upcoming programs will
point you in the right direction.

The initial training program

Once you've mastered the walking / running
technique and have become able to run for
30 minutes a day, then it's time to improve
your   performance   with   some   more
challenging types of workouts. Here is a
simple weekly training program that can
increase your stamina in the first few weeks

after the initial Walk to Run method. You can follow this program for as long as your body needs to prepare for more demanding activities.

DAY	ACTIVITIES
Monday	Easy ride
Tuesday	Constant running combined with a 10 minute fartlek
Wednesday	Day of rest
Thursday	Constant slopes combined with hill climbing
Friday	Basic and endurance training
Saturday	Day of rest

Sunday	A long time

Increase your mileage

Once you are ready for longer and more demanding runs, you can start increasing your mileage. This is a basic program of how you can go 6 to 22 miles per week.

	Mon	**Mar**	**Wednesday**	**Thurs**	**Fri**	**Sat**	**Sun**	Total mileage
Week 1	2 miles	C and R Training	2 miles	rest	C and R Training	2 miles	rest	6 miles
Week 2	C and R Traini	rest	2 miles	2 miles	C and R Traini	3 miles	rest	7 miles

	ng				ng			
Week 3	3 miles	C and R Training	rest	2 miles	C and R Training	4 miles	rest	9 miles
Week 4	C and R Training	4 miles	3 miles	C and R Training	rest	4 miles	rest	11 miles
Week 5	4 miles	C and R Training	rest	5 miles	C and R Training	5 miles	rest	14 miles
Week	C and R	4 miles	4 miles	C and R	rest	6 mil	2 mil	16 miles

6	Training			Training		es	es	
Week 7	3 miles	Cand R Training	5 miles	Cand R Training	rest	8 miles	3 miles	19 miles
Week 8	Cand R Training	5 miles	4 miles	Cand R Training	rest	10 miles	3 miles	22 miles

If you start this program and see that you still can't run the mileage, don't be disappointed. Simply repeat the first four weeks 2 or three times, then restart the program.

Every second week (which means week 2, week 4, week 6 and week 8), you can replace basic and resistance training with exercises like cycling and swimming for about 30 minutes. Your core and resistance training should last 20 minutes at first, then gradually increase to 30 or sometimes 40 minutes.

Chapter 13

THE INCOMODOUS SIDE OF THE RACE

Running is a very dynamic sport that puts repetitive pressure on your body. This is great for your physical condition, your fitness, your body shape and your overall well-being. However, most runners will tell you that there is a small price to pay for receiving all of these benefits.

Once you get started with your running schedule, chances are you will experience some of the discomforts of running sooner rather than later. But don't get frustrated, as most of them are nothing to worry about.

They can also be easily prevented with decent preparation.

- Blisters.These fluid-filled blisters can be very painful and even become infected if left untreated. To prevent them, wear double-layered socks and apply petroleum jelly to vulnerable areas such as the heel.
- Runner's Nipple. If you wear loose-fitting shirts for running, repetitive rubbing could cause irritation and bleeding around or on both nipples. To avoid this, wear running clothes. You can also apply petroleum jelly for prevention.
- Runner's tip.This is caused by bleeding that occurs under the nail due to the use of unsupported shoes. Make sure you try on your running shoes in the afternoon when your feet are swollen.
- Chest pain.This is very common among beginners who set unrealistic goals. Gradually build your running schedule

and move on to a more challenging workout when you're really ready.

 Cramps. Cramps occur due to excessive muscle contraction. TO prevent this from happening, try some massage techniques (later in this chapter).

 DOMS.Delayed onset of muscle pain occurs when a person is not physically prepared for training. That's why warm-up and cool-down exercises are essential.

INJURIES WHILE RUNNING

No matter how experienced you are, running injuries are a by-product of the pressure exerted on the body by this dynamic physical activity. That said, it's important that you are familiar with the most common injuries runners suffer from, so you can detect their symptoms in time, take the right treatment, and avoid complications.

Lumbar back pain.This is very common and can happen due to many factors like improper shape, worn shoes, uneven surfaces, etc. You will most likely feel a stiffness in your lower back that spreads to your thigh and gets worse when you start running. It is best to stop exercising for a couple of days until the inflammation subsides. If the pain does not go away or becomes more severe, contact your doctor.

Muscle tear or muscle tear.Muscle strain or strain is caused by a sudden, strong contraction (such as a sudden change in speed). Your muscles will become red, swollen and you will most likely feel pangs of pain. If such a thing happens, stop your training and consult a doctor. _Bursitis_. Bursae are the fluid-filled sacs that act as "cushions" between bones and tendons. Repetitive friction can cause inflammation and will result in a painful condition called bursitis. You can detect this injury by knowing the symptoms of tenderness and pain around the bursa area. If this occurs, stop exercising and contact your doctor.

  Runner's knee. Runner's knee occurs when tendons are tense or muscles are too weak. It causes severe pain in the front of the knee that gets worse when walking up and down stairs or pressing the kneecap. There may also be swelling. The best solution is to rest, hold back a

  ice pack and leg lifts. If that doesn't help and your knee still hurts after 10 days, contact your doctor.

Shin Splinths. Shins usually occur when you start running without warming up the muscles. Symptoms are a dull ache in the inside of the shin that increases during exercise. This is usually not dangerous and can be easily treated with a bag of ice cubes and rest, but if the pain doesn't go away after 2 weeks, you should see a doctor.

Achilles Tendonpathetic. This is characterized by Achilles tendon swelling and pain and occurs due to excessive stress on the leg. The only thing you can do is stop your training and seek medical help.

Knee Lifire injuries. When a sudden twisting motion occurs, one of the four ligaments in the knee can be easily broken or sprained. Symptoms are pain and swelling around the knee. If you do detect these symptoms, we advise you not to try to treat them yourself, but to seek medical help immediately.

Iotibial band Syndrome. The ITB (iotibial band) is a very similar structure to the tendon and is found from the pelvis to just below the knee. Repeated knee flexion can sometimes result in overuse of the ITB and cause an inflammation known as ITB syndrome. The first symptom is pain on the outside of the knee. Swelling and tenderness may also occur. See your doctor and don't leave your leg untreated.

Chapter 14

KEEP MOTIVATION ALIVE

Living at this fast, modern pace when distractions seem to lurk from every angle, you need strong willpower to hold on to your running shoes. Here are some tips that can help you keep that motivational spark alive that will inspire you to regularly go out for a run.

View. The best way to work hard to achieve a goal is to visualize the results. If your goal is to run a marathon, imagine doing it. Imagine enduring such a challenging and challenging task and having the physical condition to complete it. This will keep you motivated to train and even increase mileage as your performance progresses.

Be realistic. Always set realistic goals for yourself to avoid disappointment. No one has gone from being a couch potato to a marathon runner, and neither have you. Make sure you gradually increase the time and distance and be realistic about how much you can actually endure.

Reward yourself. Like a child who is expecting a sweet gift when he does something good, this way you can give yourself progress. Try adding rewards next to each goal. For example, if I can run 5km this week, I'll buy those fancy running shoes I saw the other day. Again, stay realistic and avoid being disappointed.

Go explore. People usually stop running because after a while it becomes a boring business. Make sure this doesn't happen to you. To avoid getting tired of your surroundings, be sure to change your running route. Go to new and unknown places where running can be just like exploring.

Listening to music. Good music can fuel your body and give you the energy to run. Create a special playlist of any songs you think might distract you from thinking about taking a break while running.

Register for a race. Finally, signing up for a race seems to be the best motivational indicator, especially if you are competitive by nature. Knowing that you have to train to become able to endure a race will keep you from fatigue and give you the strength to go another minute, another mile.

Conclusion

Running is a great sport that more and more people are practicing these days. It's simple and easy to do, and you don't need fancy equipment aside from a good pair of running shoes. Without a doubt, running makes people healthier, happier and more self-confident. It makes them realize that they can accomplish things they might have thought were out of their reach. If a constant habit is taken, running will continue to provide great benefits and a deep sense of fulfillment throughout the person's life.

To function properly and safely, be aware of the guidelines to follow and precautions to take, as discussed extensively in this book. Keep them in mind while you run and have fun! Good luck in your next races!